JAINA KIRTTI – STAMBHA
OF
CHITTORGADH

(c. 1300 A.D.)
(The Form and the Idea)

Prof. R. Nath

CONTENTS

Dedication

I dedicate this work to the memory of my grand-mother (**Amma**), who was an embodiment of love, affection and kindness; selfless devotion and sacrifice; forbearance and sincerity; hard-work; indefatigable courage; simplicity of expression; and resolution and firmness. After she was widowed at the tender age of 27, she devoted herself to Jainism and worshipped at the Shital Nath Digambar Jain Temple, Roshan Mohalla Agra, for more than 65 years and died, almost a centurion, in 1970. She was an ardent Jaina who not only believed in its tenets but also practised them in life with characteristic sincerity, boldness, dignity and grace and it was owing to her since my early childhood that I was acquainted with the basic things of this ancient faith. To me, she was more than a mother; in fact, she did more. She regulated our conduct, looked after our health, an excellent Vaidya as she was, and above all, moulded our character. To her, I owe my interest in and regard for these grand sacred relics.

— **R. Nath**

LIST OF ILLUSTRATIONS

Figures

Plates

PREFACE

The Jaina Kīrttistambha of Chittorgadh (c. 1300 A.D.) is not only an exquisite work of art and a unique architectural relic of an age, it also symbolises an ancient thought which has made it what it is. A study of its **'IDEA'** as much as its **'FORM'** is essentially needed to understand its real significance and importance to the People whose heritage it is. Unfortunately, its Meaning-and-Symbolism has been forgotten. Without this knowledge, it is of no use to worship a thing ritualistically. Without a continuous process of theorisation and intellectualism, Culture goes on to loose its purpose and raison d'etre and is reduced to a dead weight which any new generation can disown and discard, as has often happened in the History of Mankind. It is only knowledge which co-relates the People and their Cultural Heritage, more so in this age when the 'Oral Tradition' is gradually dying out and we have almost entirely to depend on the **'Written Tradition'**.

Accordingly, the 'Form' and 'Idea' of the Jaina Kīrttistambha of Chittorgadh (**JKS**) have been studied in this small monograph. Its Chapter—1 briefly describes its Architecture, while the Epigraphic data related to its construction and restorations has been discussed in Chapter—2. The other two chapters are interpretative, discussing its 'Architectural Derivation' and 'Meaning and Symbolism' respectively. The text is designed to be brief to make it most easily readable and the basic data, epigraphical and textual (e.g. on Samavasarana, Aṣṭāpada,

Merugiri and Nandīśvara-Dwīpa) has been documented in 14 appendices listed under two heads, and 2 tables describing the characteristic features of Ancient Pillars and Ancient Structures. In essence, it is an enumeration of the **THOUGHT** which has gone into its making as such. Seventeen figures (line-drawings of plans, section and elevation) and 24 halftone plates have been used to illustrate the work.

It was originally published in 1994, this is its revised and updated addition.

ISBN 81 – 85105 – 22 – 7

Mob. 08278687716, 9413617454
profnath@gmail.com
www.rnath.in

Professor (Dr) R Nath,
M.A., Ph.D., D.Litt
(Retired Professor & Head of the Deptt
of History & Indian Culture, University of
Rajasthan JAIPUR)
'Tapasya'
7, Gulab Bari Enclave
(Behind Asharam Chaudhary)
Gulab Bari
AJMER 305007 (Rajasthan, INDIA)

1

Architecture of
The Jaina Kirtti-Stambha (JKS)

THE Jainas adopted the idea of the Vedic *Skambha*, *Yūpa* and the Vaiṣṇava *Dhvaja-Stambha* in the form of *Mānasa-Stambha*, or *Mānavaka-Stambha*, or, more popularly, **Māna-Stambha**, which was raised as a votive column in front of the *Çaitya* (Jina-Temple). Such pillars were originally surmounted by *Dharma-Çakra* symbol, as is depicted on the *Āyāgapaṭṭ* of Sīha Vaṇika in the Mathura Museum. Later, they had images on top and at the base and invariably faced the Jaina temple. The *Ādipurāṇa* of Jinasena speaks of '*Mānasa-stambhas*' upon which images of Jinas were placed.[1] At still a later date, the *Mānasa-stambha*, as the Jaina *dhvaja-stambha* was named, was crowned by symbol of the particular Jina whose shrine it faced.[2] Several inscriptions of Chittorgadh, of the period from 13th to 15th century A.D., record the construction and consecration of *Māna-Stambha*, viz. The **Jaina-Kīrttistambha;** these are also referred to it as Kīrttistambha, as shall be discussed hereafter.

The JKS preceded the *Kīrttistambha* (KS) of Maharana Kumbha, also situated at Chittorgadh, by about two centuries and, as an ideal precursor, it inspired the latter in a large degree. Of particular interest are such common features in both these structures as :

    (1)   a square plan with *karnikās, bhadras* and other horizontal and vertical mouldings;

    (2)   an internal stairway (*sopāna*);

    (3)   stationing of sectarian and ornamental sculptures on the exterior; and

    (4)   orientation towards the South.

Tod noticed it in the *Annals* as follows[3]:—

"Higher up and, nearly about the centre, is a remarkable square pillar, called the Khawasan-sthamba (column)[4]. It is 75 1/2' in height, 35' in diameter at the base and 15' at the top, and covered with Jaina figures. It is very ancient and I found a fragment of an inscription at its base, which shows that it was dedicated to Adinath, the first of the 24 Jain pontiffs:

    'By Sri Adinath, and the twentyfour Jineswara, Pundarikaksha, Ganesa, Surya and the nine planets, may you be preserved. S. 952 (A. D. 896)[5] Baisakh (sudi) the 30th, Guruwar (Thursday)'."

It is unlikely that this epigraph belonged to the Jaina Kīrttistambha which cannot be assigned, stylistically and otherwise, to such an early date.

Fergusson referred to it as 'Sri Allata's Tower', 75' in height and : "adorned with sculpture and mouldings from base to the summit. It stands on a basement of 20' square and 9' high with a stair on the south side, leading to the doorway which is 6'-2" above the platform. The shaft of the tower is 12'-10" square below and is four storeys high[6] to the open canopy of 12 pillars, the floor of which is 64'-2" (high) from the ground. An inscription once existed lying near its base, which is said to have given its date as A.D. 895, though the slab has now been lost. This however is much too early a date for the style of the structure and the discovery of a reference in a manuscript poem of late date ascribing it to Kumārapāla of Gujarat (A. D. 1142-73), though the style is in no way inconsistent with such a date, as it is unsupported by any nearly contemporary record, is of no historical value. The tower belongs to the 12th century......dedicated to Ādināth."[7]

He also made the curious comment: "and nude figures of them are repeated some hundreds of times on the face of the tower, distinguishing it as a Digamber monument, whilst Kumārapāla was a Swetambar."[8]

It is a pity that he did not go into the meaning and purpose of such a magnificent structure as this. Did the people raise it out of fun ?

Percy Brown also described it, instead of venturing to define it : "Of the monumental towers there is one exceptionally well-designed example in a style related to that of the Solanki period and dating from the twelfth century (A.D.). This Jayastambha at Chitor was probably a 'Pillar of Fame' set up before a Jain Temple which has now disappeared. A temple stands besides the tower but it is a fourteenth century production, evidently built on the site of the original edifice. The tower rises to some eighty feet in height and is in eight stories, the active principles of this fine conception plainly showing that the craftsmen were by no means slaves to the temple-type but could, when required, create equally beautiful buildings of another kind and for another purpose. Its foundation is a simple platform from which mount the spreading mouldings of the basement to support the most prominent feature, corresponding the mandovara or wall-space in the temple design, a protecting storey, consisting of tabernacles and niches containing figures. Above this the stories recede or expand in measured alternation to finish an open pillared pavilion with a pyramidal roof which forms the summit. Each storey is enriched with mouldings, balconied-windows, turrets and other architectural motifs, the whole presenting an appearance of animated variety yet all in perfect unison, a subtle blending of qualities of beauty and strength."[9]

Besides being unmindful of its raison d'etre, vague as to its period and uncertain about its builder, Percy Brown erred in several other respects. 'Pillar of Fame' is a literal translation of **'kīrttistambha'** which does not convey its meaning correctly. A brief architectural survey of its form and an analysis of its idea are called for.

Entirely built of yellowish, golden coloured, sandstone, it has six storeys (and consequently six floors) **(Figs. 1 to 8)** which measure as follows :

Height (excluding ceiling)	Across in the curvilinear plan
(1) 12' — 2" (3.71 m)	— 20' — 5" (6.22 m)
(2) 10' — 11" (3.30 m)	— 14' — 6" (4.42 m)
(3) 9' — 5" (2.87 m)	— 13' — 6" (4.11 m)
(4) 8' — 0" (2.44 m)	— 10' — 9" (3.25 m)
(5) 6' — 10" (2.08 m)	— 11' — 6" (3.51 m)
(6) 14' — 11" (4.55 m)	— 14' — 6" (4.42 m)
(including *sikhara*)	

The total height of the *JKS* including the *jagatī* is 80'-5" (24.51 m). It is square with a *dvi-aṅga plan (having one karṇa between the two bhadras)*, which is maintained all along the elevation, measuring 20'-5" (6.22 m) across at the base and 14'-6" (4.42 m) at the top, diminishing or enlarging in span in various storeys as it rises in accordance with its beautiful design which is a masterpiece in the whole range of the Indian Art **(Plates 1 to 24),** not owing to any sculpturesque decor but because of the way it has been conceived **architecturally** as a whole.

The *jagatī* (main plinth or platform) is 7'-10" (2.39 m) high, having stairs on the south side. It has a *grāsapaṭṭī (rows of kīrttimukhas)* on the border, rotating on all sides and an empty *rathikā* (ornamental framed niche) in the middle of each side. The *JKS* faces south and it is on this side that it has, at a considerable height, a small rectangular door, approachable by stairs, giving access into the interior which is planned only to accommodate, very cleverly, the stairways which connect one floor with the other. The interior is plain and except for the provision of a **sopāna** (stairway), it has no other function, while in Kumbha's **kīrttistambha** built here after about 150 years, interior has been specifically planned for the depiction of hundreds of sculptures of divinities around the main shaft.

The *JKS* is not something different from the Temple (Hindu or Jaina Prāsāda), but a form of the Temple itself with *pītha, maṇḍovara* and other accessories bearing images and sculptures depicted on the four zones of each *karṇa* between the two *bhadras* (sides) of its *dvi-anga* plan.[10] Its *pītha,* like the *jagatī,* is extraordinarily high and, obviously, the emphasis has been bestowed on the elevation *(ūrdhvacchanda)* rather than on the horizontal axis *(talacchanda);* it has been designed exactly like the *pītha* of the Temple and it has such traditional mouldings as *bhiṭṭ, jādyakumbha, karṇaka, grasapaṭṭī* (showing rows of *kīrttimukhas*), *gajathara* (showing elephants) and *narathara* depicting **loka-jīwana** (scenes from life) including battle and hunting scenes, processions and religious ceremonies.

Like the Temple, the *JKS* also has a distinct *maṇḍovara* in three distinct parts : *vedibandha, jaṁghā* and *varaṇḍikā.* The *vedibandha* has the traditional *khuraka, kumbhaka* having Śāsana-Devīs (Yakṣiṇīs) in *āsana* posture contained in beautiful ornamental arch-shaped *rathikās* on the *bhadras* and *karṇas* and *kalaśa* mouldings. Exquisitely designed *toraṇālayas* (deep, sunk niches with *illikā-toraṇas*) have been set on the *bhadras* (i.e.on all the front sides) on the *jaṁghā* part containing kāyotsarga images of the tīrthankara Ādinātha. The *jaṁgha*, as usual, has been most profusely and tastefully ornamented. *Sthānaka* sculptures of Hindu divinities as Brahmā and Śiva have been shown, of course ornamentally, on the *karṇas* on this part. Surprisingly, while Bhairava (a ferocious and violent form of the Śiva) images have been repeated, there is no Viṣṇu. Was this scheme worked out to keep the pre-dominant Śaivites in good humour, Chittorgadh being a great Śaiva *tīrtha*, and Mewar a Śaiva country ? Ornamental sculptures of beautiful *devāṅganās* in graceful postures have also been used inside the *karṇas*, four on each, there thus being 16 in all which set offers an extremely interesting study of formal art within the forum of a sacred one.

A *śikhara* does not take over above the *khuraçhādya* and, instead, a *sahastrakūṭa* depicting series of miniature *āsana* tīrthankaras has been carved on all sides *(bhadras* and *karṇas)*. Above it, on the *bhadras*, are set beautifully designed *vātāyanas* with *āsanapaṭṭikās*, miniature pillars, brackets, *chhajjās* and *sīrṣas* (which resemble *śukanāsas*). These *vātāyanas* which look like *jharokhās* provide rhythmic shadows along with the elevational axis. On the *karṇas* are ornamental *śṛṅgas* or miniature *śikharas* which seem to provide a logical superstructure to the four *karṇas* of the *dvi-aṅga* plan of the building; it is in them that the idea of the temple elevation formally culminates. These *vātāyanas* have in fact been provided like the traditional *pārśvalindas* of the Temple and it seems that while the architect was composing it with the traditional constituents of the Temple, he did not forget its characteristic features to incorporate into its fabric.

Several other mouldings, one showing series of very bold *kīrtti-mukhas* in high relief, projecting forward prominently, supersede this storey on the elevation. The superstructure resting on several corbelled mouldings, each upper course projecting forward is, in fact, an open *maṇḍapa* (pillared pavilion) of 12 tastefully designed pillars. It has *illikā toraṇas* on the *bhadras* (sides) and is protected above by a rotating *chhajjā*. Its pillars and *toraṇas* are typical of the exquisite Jaina Art. It does not have the traditional *ekāṇḍaka* or *anekāṇḍaka* Nāgara *śikhara* which roofed the *mūlaprāsāda* of the Temple, and, instead, it has a *Samvaraṇā* (stepped pyramidal; tiered) roof (which traditionally roofed the main *maṇḍapa*) crowned by an *āmalaka* and *kalaśa*.[11] It is here that it has differed from the traditional scheme but, in any case, it is a perfectly befitting superstructure.

Precisely, the *JKS* is a form of the Temple planned and laid out vertically on the *ūrdhvaçchanda* (elevation) and while the Temple constituents incorporated in its body-fabric denoted the Ancient symbolic **structures** like Meru and Samavasaraṇa, its verticality denoted the Ancient symbolic **pillars** like *Skambha*, *Kīrttistambha* and *Mānastambha*. This has made the difference and created a little mystery about its form and idea.

It is necessary to go into some fundamentals of the *JKS* to be able to make an estimate of the inspiration which the builders of the *KS* of Maharana Kumbha derived from it. As a large number of religious and literary works and epigraphs show, Chittorgadh (Citrakūṭa) was an important seat of Jainism since ancient times. "Citrakūṭa-Utpatti-Prabandha" in the *Purātana-Prabandha-Sangraha* gives the legend of the origin of Chittorgadh, which shows that Jainism owned it as an important Tīrtha, and as the 'Chittor-Caitya-Paripāṭī-Dvaya' indicates, numerous Jaina temples were built here from time to time and once they numbered 32 with nearly eightthousand images in consecration.[12] As late as the 15th century A.D. the whole Mewar (Medapāṭa) country, crowned by Citrakūṭa, was adorned by temples and *kīrttistambhas* as the Mahāvīra Temple Praśasti composed in V.S. 1495/1438 A.D. affirms:—

स्थानस्थानविराजमानविशदप्रासाददम्भोदतो ।

यो देशानितरान्विजित्य *विजयस्तम्भम्समुत्तम्भयेत्* ॥ ७ ॥[13]

It is noteworthy that these *stambhas* were called **'Vijayastambha'** because Jainism had conquered the Land and the People, where they were raised in each case. No military action is implied; it is the conquest of the 'Saddharma' (सद्धर्म) i.e. Jainism, which is denoted by the nomenclature 'Vijayastambha'. This has been further elucidated in the same *prasasti—*

रागद्वेषजितो जिनस्य *विजयस्तम्भौ किमुत्तम्भितौ* ॥ ९३ ॥

(These victory towers were raised in the honour of the Jina who had triumphed over worldly attachment and hatred).[14]

                                         ✱ ✱ ✱

1. The **JKS** full view from East

2. The **JKS** with the Mahāvīra Temple, from East (towards South)

3. The **JKS** from East (Jagatī and Pīṭha)

4. The **JKS** from East (Jaṁghā)

5. The **JKS** from East (Maṇḍapa & Vātāyana)

6. The **JKS** from East (Maṇḍapa & Superstructure)

7. The **JKS** full view from East

8. The **JKS** superstructure from North-East

9. The **JKS** from North (Jagatī & Pīṭha)

10. The **JKS** from North (towards East) (Pīṭha & Jaṁghā)

11. The **JKS** from North (Superstructure)

12. The **JKS** from North (towards West) (details of Pīṭha & Jaṁghā)

13. The **JKS** from West (Jagatī & Pīṭha)

14. The **JKS** from West (Jaṁghā Sculptures)

15. The **JKS** from West (Details of Mouldings)

16.   The **JKS** from West (Details of Mouldings)

17.   The **JKS** from South (Pīṭha & Jaṁghā)

18. The **JKS** from South (Pīṭha, Jaṁghā & Maṇḍapa)

19. The **JKS** from South (Details of the Jaṃghā)

20. The **JKS** from South (Details of Mouldings)

21. The **JKS** from South (Maṇḍapa & Vātāyanas)

22. The **JKS** from South (Superstructure)

23. The **JKS** from South (Sculptures & Mouldings)

24. The **JKS** from South-East with Mahavira Temple, full view

2

Epigraphical Data

THE epigraphical data related to the *JKS*[15] can be summarised, in order to fix up its origin and chronology, as follows:—

(A) The epigraph preserved in the Topkhana Museum Chittorgadh dated in V.S. 1357/1300 A.D. Phalguna Sudi (?) recording the installation of a Māna-stambha or *kīrttistambha* viz. the *JKS* by Jījā (Jījāka) whose father Nāya built Chandraprabha temple at Chittorgadh; it was completed by Jījā's son Punyasingh and the consecration ceremony was performed by Dharmacandra of Mūlasaṅgha.[16] The epigraph has 29 *ślokas* in 25 lines, in Sanskrit.

(B) Two epigraphs preserved in the Victoria Hall Museum Udaipur, recording the installation of a *stambha* = Māna-stambha = *kīrttistambha* at Chittorgadh by Jījā (Jījāka) son of Sāh Nāya of the Bagherawāla caste.[17] The operative part reads as follows:—

आकारैर्वियुतं युतं च----------

------- स्वमहसि स्वार्थप्रकाशात्मके

मज्जंतो निरूपाख्यमोघचिदचिन्मोक्षार्थितीर्थक्षिप: ।

कृत्वा नाद्य:

------- स्थितिकृते स्वर्गापवर्गात्तये ।

य: प्राज्ञैरनुमीयते सुकृतिना जीजेन निर्मापित

स्तंभ: सै--------

-------- सुभालोकैर्न कैरंच्यते ॥

बघेरवालजातीय सा: नाय सुत जीजाकेन

स्तंभ: कारापित: ॥ शुभं भवतु ॥

This is contemporaneous to No. (A) above.

(C) The Chittorgadh *prasasti* recording the completion and consecration of the Māna-stambha viz. the *JKS* at Chittorgadh by Pūrṇasiṁha who is also mentioned as Puṇyasiṁha, contemporarily, i. e. c.1300 A.D.[18] It contains *slokas* 21 to 45.

(D) The inscription preserved at Chittorgadh containting 12 *slokas* dealing with Jaina devotional worship related to the Nirvāṇa of 24th Tīrthankara Mahāvīra. Its colophon[19]:—

तेनसुवानंतजिने (श्वरा) णां मुनिगणानां च (निर्वाण)

स्थानानि निवृत्यै (वा) पांतु संघं जीजान्वितं सदा ॥

records the well-being of the Jaina-Saṁgha along with Jījā and is, therefore, contemporary to the previous inscriptions.

(E) 'Citrakūṭa-Durga-Mahāvīra-Prāsāda-Prasasti', the manuscript copy of which is preserved in the Bhandarkar Oriental Research Institute Poona, recording that the Mahāvīra Temple was rebuilt by Guṇarāja and his sons placed a new image of Vardhamāna in it in 1485/1428.[20] The *prasasti* was composed in 1495/1438 by Cāritra-Ratna-Gaṇi, pupil of Somasundara who enlightened Guṇarāja. It was calligraphed by a Jati named Saṁvaigaja and engraved by Nārada, son of Sūtradhāra Lakṣa. The *prasasti* was copied in 1508/1451. The *prasasti* begins with obeisance to Śrī-Sarvajña. The first verse is devoted to the praise of Bhāratī, the goddess of speech. Verses 2-6 invoke the blessings of the 1st, 16th, 22nd, 23rd and 24th tīrthankaras respectively. Verse-7 speaks of the Medapāṭa (Mewar) country and its stupendous edifices. Verses 8-17 deal with Guhila and his descendants upto Mokal. Verses 18-25 are devoted to the praise of the exploits of Kumbha. Verses 26-75 deal with the family of Viśāla of the Oswal caste in whose lineage was born Guṇarāja who rebuilt the Mahāvīra temple. Verses 76-85 describe the order of pontifical succession of the Jaina Tapagachcha. The last verses from 86 to 104 deal with the main subject and record the reconstruction of the temple and it is in this reference that the *JKS* has been described.[21]

(F) Nandgaon (Karanja) image inscription of V.S. 1541/1484 A.D. recording the reconstruction of the temple of Supārśvanātha and consecration of the image by Puṇasī, Dharmasī and Devasī (Pūrṇasiṁha, Dharmasiṁha and Devasiṁha respectively) being the 10th descendants in line of Jījā (Jījāka) who installed the **Kīrttistambha** in front of the temple of Candraprabha at Chittorgadh[22] :

मेदपाटदेशे चित्रकूटनगरे
श्रीचन्द्रप्रभजिनेन्द्र–
चैत्यालयस्याग्रे निजभुजोपार्जितवित्तबलेन
श्री कीर्तिस्तम्भः आरोपक साह जीजा ।

This data confirms, without the least doubt, the following facts :—

(1) Śreṣṭhī Nāya, father of Jījāka of the Bagherwāla caste, built Caityālaya (Jina-Mandira) of Candraprabha (8th Tīrthankara) at Chittorgadh, presumably in the last quarter of the 13th century A.D.

(2) Jījā (Jījāka) son of the same Nāya, of the Bagherwāla caste, commissioned the *JKS* in front of this temple of Candraprabha, towards the end of the 13th century A.D.

(3) The *JKS* was completed by Jījāka's son (Pūrṇasiṁha) (Punyasiṁha) and the consecration ceremony was performed by the Jaināċārya Dharmaċandra of the Mūlasaṁgha on (?) day of Sudi (Śukla Pakṣa) of the month of Phālguna, in the year V.S. 1357/1300 A.D.

(4) Chittorgadh having been devastated and its temples destroyed during the Khaljī occupation, A.D. 1303 to 1313, need arose

to restore them and consequently one Guṇarāja started restoration and reconstruction of the temple which had originally been built by Nāya, during the reign of Mokal. Presumably, it was originally a Śvetāmbara temple; Guṇarāja intended to consecrate it to Digambara worship and dedicate it to the 24th Tīrthankara Vardhamāna Mahāvīra. But he left it incomplete. His sons completed it and consecrated in it a new image of Vardhamāna in 1485/1428. Its praśasti was composed during the reign of Kumbha in 1495/1438 by Cāritra-Ratna-Gaṇi, pupil of Somasundara who had enlightened Guṇarāja.

(5) To the south of the Mahāvīra temple was another Caityālaya (Jinālaya, Jaina temple) built by Porwāl Kumārapāla; and to its north was the temple built by Oswāl Chacha, son of Tejā. The situation of the temples along with the *JKS* may thus be drawn and shown in **Fig. 9.**

(6) The *JKS* also seems to have been restored simultaneously by Guṇarāja, or by Kumbha the Ādivarāha, or quite likely by the descendants of Jījāka who, as the Nandgaon (Karanja) image inscription shows, had not forgotten this memorial of their 10th ancestor.

It may be reiterated that these inscriptions e. g. verses 7 and 21-23 etc. of the Mahāvīra-Prāsāda-Praśasti, mention *vijayastambhas* and *kīrttistambhas* synonymously **as a commemorative rather than as a votive column** but in no case it was a military relic or memorial of a mundane thing. The same inscription explicitly defines *'kīrttistambha'* thus :—

रागद्वेषजितो जिनस्य विजयस्तम्भौ किमुत्तम्भितौ

पारावारदुरन्तदुर्गतियुगोत्ताराय सेतु किमु ।

किं वोच्यैस्त्रिदिवापवर्गगमने निश्रेणिदण्डाविभौ

कीर्तिस्तम्भममुं च वीक्ष्य विदधत्येवं विकल्पान्त्र के॥ ९३ ॥

(On perceiving this temple of Mahāvīra built by Guṇarāja, and the Kīrttistambha, viz. the *JKS* adjoining it, people began to surmise that these towers of victory were raised in honour of the Jina who had triumphed over worldly attachment and hatred; or these were bridges for crossing the boundless ocean; or these are stairs of the ladder to go to the Heaven (Apavarga, Nirvāṇa). The people who look at the Kīrttistambha, viz. the *JKS* thus surmise).

This gives an important clue that a **Jaina kīrttistambha** was also called Vijayastambha not because it commemorated the victory of an army through a fight on the battlefield after a colossal bloodshed and violence (हिंसा), but the victory of Jainism over the Land and the People and the victory over humanly passions and attachment, hence the expression : रागद्वेष जितो जिनस्य विजयस्तम्भौ किमुत्तम्भितौ । It is Vijayastambha because it denotes victory of Saddharma (सद्धर्म). The Vaiṣṇava **kīrttistambha was also called vijayastambha exactly with the same meaning in view.**

A Kumārapāla has been mentioned in the verse-95 of this inscription as the one who built a Jaina-Caitya on the south side of the *JKS*. This Kumārapāla has nothing to do with Kumārapāla Solankī of Gujarat and it is absurd to identify the former with the latter, as it has been sometimes attempted.

***

3

Sopāna-Paddhati & Architectural Derivation

THE most important reference of this praśasti is सोपानपद्धतिभिमामधिरूह्य भव्याः स्वर्गापवर्गभवनेषु सुखंरमध्वम् (verse-94) (O, pious people, ascend its stairs, reach the Heaven and live in the gorgeous Heavenly Tabernacle with perpetual Bliss). It records, explicitly, that the *JKS* was built on the सोपानपद्धति, i. e. **with an inner stairway,** as if to lead to the Heaven above. So far the *kīrttistambhas* and the *dhvajastambhas* were all monolithic stone pillars, the only exception being the **Ubha-Dīwala** *stambha* of Nagari near Chittorgadh which was built of blocks of stone leaving a hollow space inside. Though, of course, stairs were not there, it was suggestive of such a feature to any creative architect. The *JKS* is the first of the Hindu *stambhas* to contain an inner stairway. **Sopāna-Paddhati** reference alludes to, and explains, this mystery.

It may be noted that the 12th century Vāstu-text : *Aparājitapṛcchā* prescribed things for the construction of the *kīrttistambhas* with reference to the laying out of the *Bhūdhara* and *Hemakūṭa* types of cities (Sūtras-70 and 71 respectively) and also along with the description of *'Dhvajas'* (Sūtra-145).[23]

The last one contains allusion to an inner, spiralling stairway, e.g.

पीठबन्धोपरि कुर्यादूर्ध्वं चैवं तु मेखला ।

(AP. CXLV. 18).[24]

When this reference of *Mekhalā* (मेखला) of such a standard text as the *AP*, is read with the *Sopāna-Paddhati* (सोपान-पद्धति) of the aforesaid *prasasti*, there remains no doubt as to the provision of a stairway which rotates or spirals inside the *kīrttistambha* from the bottom to the top and, as it seems, the **Ubha-Dīwāla** structure, and the Sāstric dictum were enough to guide the architect to plan and provide it in the *JKS*.

The multi-storeyed *JKS* of Chittorgadh with a square plan and an inner stairway is the first example of its type in the Hindu Architecture, the *KS* of Maharana Kumbha being the second, though a far more refined, enlarged and sophisticated one. Its was a later development and the sources of its architectural inspiration may be varied and it is necessary to review other preceding structures of this class.

The ancient Assyrians built '**Ziggurat**' (Jārūka, जारूक) which was a square, multi-storeyed open structure with receding tiers in which series of stairs were used. A Ziggurat was intact at Khorsabad as late as the second half of the 12th century A.D.[25] It had seven storeys, round which a gentle, open staircase rotated. The '**Sawāmi**' or towers at the four corners of the ancient Temenos' of Damascus were also square with receding storeys. Temenos' was originally a Syrian temple which had been converted into church. When al-Wālid (705-15 A.D.) built the Great Mosque on the site of the 'Temenos', the four towers, viz. the 'Sawami' at the corners were not disturbed. In fact, one was used for giving the call to prayer (āzān). It had an inner stairway. Several other pre-Muslim towers which have come down to us are also square and multi-storeyed with receding tiers; they also have inner stairs. They all belong to the same class. It may be noted that these were essentially watch-towers and, like the 'Sawāmi' of Damascus, occupied corners or edges of the complex to which they were attached. They were strictly functional. That this structure also had a symbolic meaning related to the mythology of the people who raised it has not been made out so far.

The 'Mālwīya' or **'Manār al-Mālwīya',** the spiral minaret of the Great Mosque of Samarra, built by Khalifah al-Mutawakkil (c. 847 A.D.) is an altogether different structure. It stands outside the mosque, exactly facing it, on a square platform and rises to a height of 164' (about 50 metres). It has a circular plan; but there are no stairs and, instead, a 7½' (2.29 metres) wide ramp spirals round the main shaft in an anti-clock wise direction. Obviously, its inspiration was not derived either from the Ziggurat or the 'Sawāmi'. It was an experiment to erect a symbolic structure in front of the place of worship in imitation of the *Dhvajastambha*,[26] and the architect introduced 'ramp' as an innovation mainly because he was not using a monolithic stone pillar but working on masonry. It fulfilled more a constructional than a functional need.

The plan and design of Minaret developed through the course of more than three centuries in the region which extended from Damascus to Delhi. However, as the numerous extant structures show, e.g. the Tower of Damghan (1058 A.D.), Minaret of Daulatabad near Balkh (1108-9 A.D.), Tower of Bostam (1313 A.D.), Minaret of Jam (late 12th century A.D.), minarets of Ghazni (early 12th century A.D.) and Minaret of Khwajah Siah Posh (c. 1150 A.D.), it retained some fundamental features, viz.

   (1)   whether round or star-shaped, it was essentially built on a circular plan;
   (2)   it was made of brick-masonry;
   (3)   it had an internal stairway; and

(4)   it was a commemorative, roughly, a memorial pillar and the original symbolic meaning of the Mālwīya of Samarra was soon forgotten or given up.

Except that it was made of blocks of stone, instead of brick, the Quṭb Mīnār (c. 1200-1215 A.D.) at Delhi was also built on these fundamentals.[27] It may be emphasized that it is the FIRST structure of this class consisting of free-standing detached towers. minarets and *kīrttistambhas,* in India, which has an internal spiralling stairway leading from the bottom to the top. All earlier Indian examples are stone monoliths; the only exception is the **Ubha-Dīwala** *stambha* of Nagari which is made of blocks of stone, leaving a hollow space inside, to a considerable height. With such a prominent example as the Quṭb Mīnār standing at Delhi which was also a great seat of Jainism about this time, the *Ubha-Dīwala* structure could be constructively suggestive to the architect of the *JKS* to conceive, plan, work out and bring about a rotating stairway inside his creation. The repeated allusion of this stairway of the *JKS* in the *praśasti* of V.S. 1495/1438 A.D. as leading to heaven and the specific mention of **Sopāna-Paddhati** shows that it was a new feature as far as the Hindu Architecture was concerned. It was this innovation which served as the basis for the planning and designing of the **Kīrttistambha** of Maharana Kumbha some two centuries later.

* * *

4

Meaning & Symbolism

MORE interesting and important than the sources of its architectural inspiration is the study of the meaning, symbolism and purpose of the *JKS*. Its symbolism is, truly, one of the most abstract features of Indian Art, yet it is necessary in the present context, to outline a visible caricature briefly.

It may be noted that the nomenclatures *'Mānastambha'* and *'Kīrttistambha'* have been used in the inscriptions of the *JKS* synonymously and the *JKS*, though a *caturāsra* (square) stone structure of seven storeys, with an inner spiralling stairway, has been denoted as *'Kīrttistambha'.*[28] It has also been designated as Meru : मेरु:कनकप्रभ: in the Pūrṇasiṁha-Praśasti (v. 38) and, with reference to the *JKS* and the Mahāvīra-Prāsāda, situated in close proximity,[29] the daily journey of the Sun and the rest of his horses in noon on these structures has also been mentioned : प्रासादे द्योतमानेरविरथतुरगप्राप्तविश्रान्तिकेऽस्मिन् ।[30] This confirms that the ancient idea of Vedic *skambha* and *yūpa*, and *Vaiṣṇava dhvajastambha* and *kīrttistambha* had also been incorporated in Jaina religious thought and, in fact, the Kīrttistambha's was a unitary Indian concept, common to Buddhism, Jainism and Hinduism alike.[31] Similarly, the idea of Meru and Mahāmeru constituted the basic fabric of the Jaina thought on Cosmology under such denominations as *Meru* and *Pañcameru; Nandīśvara; aṣṭapāda;* and, most important of them all, *Samavasaraṇa,* as has been elaborately described in such ancient Jaina texts as the *Tiloya-Paṇṇati* (Prākrat) (तिलोय-पण्णति = त्रैलोक्य-प्रज्ञप्ति Trailokya-Prajñapti) of Vṛṣabhācārya, the present recension of which seems to have been done by Jinasena c. 9th century A.D. Almost all Jaina texts prescribe the worship of *'Samavasaraṇa'* (समवसरण) and, for that matter, describe it architecturally to facilitate its construction. Originally, it was built by the gods-in one case by Indra, the Lord of the gods-on the nirvāṇa of the jinas and, as such, it was a funerary structure at its inception, and commemorative in implication, like the *stūpa* Later, it assumed a votive significance and was prescribed for worship, exactly like *stūpa.* It was incorporated integrally into the architecture of the Jina-Caitya (Jaina Prāsāda) as a :—

1. *caturāsra* (square) or *sarvatobhadra* (visible auspiciously on all the four sides) structure, viz. ARCHITECTURE,
2. with three *bhadrapīṭhas* (terraces) which were interconnected by series of stairways,
3. containing all the celestial and terrestrial beings of the *jagat.*

Parikara, Meru, Mahāmeru, Nadīśvara and Aṣṭapāda are the architectural variations of the same concept, which has drawn the inspiration from the basic repertoire of the Ancient Indian Thought. It was ultimately this which went into the shaping of Indian Sacred Architecture.[32]

It may also be mentioned that the third khaṇḍa of the *VDP* (on the Fine Arts) which can be assigned to the middle of the 7th century A.D., lays down theory of some structures of the same class. Thus, while, it gives the iconography of the **'Ākāśa'**[33] (आकाश) obviously as a sculpture, it describes **'Vyoman'** (व्योम) as a *caturāsra* (square) structure, like Meru, with three *bhadrapīṭhas* (terraces) depicting gods.[34] It is an Architecture. Its worship has been prescribed. It is exactly similar to the Jaina *samavasaraṇa*. Again, in a separate chapter, it describes **'Aiḍūka'** (ऐडूक) in details as an Architecture, basically being a *caturāsra* structure with *bhadrapīṭhas* and *sopānas* (stairways) containing icons, and it has also been prescribed for worship.[35] This was also originally a funerary structure. This is also similar to *samavasaraṇa;* though, of course, *Vyoman* is closer, all the three belong to the same class and have grown and developed from the same basic concept.

It may thus be deduced that, originally, this symbolism found expression in two types of relics : one, in the Vedic symbolic pillar, *skambha* (स्कम्भ), *stambha* (स्तम्भ or stabha स्तभ्), *yūpa* etc, which developed into various *dhvajastambhas, kīrttistambhas*[36] and *mānastambhas* in Brahmanical, Buddhist and Jaina religious thought and was associated in later times with the **Sūrya-Puruṣa** concept. It was a monolithic PILLAR and, hence, technically a SCULPTURE.

The other was the *stūpa, caitya, aiḍūka* etc, which was, in either case, originally functionally funerary. Basically it was commemorative and later became votive, as the *VDP* and other texts lay down. Ziggurat (Jārūka) also belonged to this class.[37] It was a structure and hence an ARCHITECTURE. Of equal antiquity, or probably of greater, is the concept of Meru (Sumeru) which symbolished *'Trailokya'* (त्रैलोक्य) or *Jagat'* (जगत्) which was a square structure with three terraces interconnected by stairways, depicting all celestial and terrestrial phenomena. To this thought belonged, essentially and fundamentally, the Jaina *Samavasaraṇa* and the allied Jaina structures, and *Vyoman* and other Brahmanical relics, as laid down by the *VDP*. All these were Architecture.

These were in practice for centuries, in fact, for several millenniums. When the things had been perfected, their standardised texts were written down, or recensions made, e.g. in the *VDP* in the middle of the 7th century A.D. and the *Tiloya-Pannati* around the 9th century A.D. The establishment of the Delhi Sultanate (1192 A.D.) and the incarnation of such structures as the Qutb Mīnār, changed the whole scene. It was necessary to review the situation and revise the symbolic things to be adjustable to the changed times. It was subsequent to this that the two types of relics, viz. one belonging to the *'Skambha'* class in the **Suçikācchanda'** and the other of the *'Meru'* class in the **'Meruçchanda'** coalesced and integrated into one and thus grew the idea of the *JKS*, during the 13th century A.D. It is as definitely a *Kīrttistambha* as certainly it is a *sarvatobhadra (çaturāsra)* **Samavasaraṇa** with several storeys (technically *bhadrapīṭhas,* terraces) interconnected by stairways, depicting celestial and terrestrial beings, in faithful adherence to the texts.

$$* * *$$

REFERENCES

1. Cf. U.P. Shah, *Studies in Jaina Art* (Banares 1955) p.60. See 'Bibliography & Notes' below.
2. Ibid, 61. There is a text: *'Māna-Stambha-Pūjā'* (ms. No. 7758) mentioned in the *Catalogue of Sanskrit and Prakrit Mss.* in the Central Provinces of Berar by Hiralal (Nagpur Govt. Press, 1926). It has yet to be studied. See Appendix-B (5) below.
3. *Annals & Antiquities of Rajasthan* (ed. W. Crooke) (Delhi 1971) Vol. III, 1822-23.
4. Tod's editor (cf. ibid) notes in ftn. 3 that this was built by Bagherwal Mahajan Jija (Jijaka) in the 12th or 13th century A.D. and that it is a Digambara monument, and could not be assigned to Kumārapāla Solankī of Gujarat (1142-73 A.D.) who was a Śvetāmbara.
5. Correctly, 895 A.D.
6. There are six storeys.
7. *History of Indian & Eastern Architecture* (Delhi 1967) Vol. I, 57-59.
8. Ibid, 59.
9. *Indian Architecture* (Buddhist & Hindu Period) (Bombay, 1971) Vol. I, p.123.
10. On the growth of the Hindu temple, reference may be made to this author's *The Art of Khajuraho* (New Delhi, 1980) pp.15-17.

11. The superstructure of the *JKS* was damaged by lightening. It was restored and the *JKS* was thoroughly repaired by Maharana Fatehsingh (1885-1929 A.D.) at a cost of Rs. 80,000/-.

12. For details of the history of Jainism at Chittorgadh, reference may be made to this author's *Antiquities of Chittorgadh*, Vol. I (Jaipur, 1984) pp.2-20.

13. D. R. Bhandarkar, *Journal of the Bombay Branch of the Royal Asiatic Society (JBBRAS)*, Vol. 23, p.50.

14. The word **'vijaya'** is used in a religious sense generally in the Jaina inscriptions. See for example the mention: चिर विजयतां श्रीशान्तिनाथ चैत्यं कारयिता च । in *Prachin-Lekha-Sangraha* (ed. Vijaydharma Suri, Bhavnagar 1929) Part-I, inscription No. 118 dated in V.S. 1478/1421 A.D. on the Maṅgala Caitya of Jawar (Udaipur). In fact, it was the style of the composers of Sanskrit epigraphs and panygyrics to use the word 'vijaya' in the sense of auspiciousness and prosperity in their compositions. The phrase विजयराज्ये has been popularly used along with the names of Kumbha in a large number of his epigraphs, e.g. श्रीकुंभकर्णविजयराज्ये (Padrana epigraph of 1490/1433, cf. *RB*, VIII.1-2, p.76; Delwara Mewar epigraph of 1491/1434 cf. *Nahar*, II. 256 and श्रीकुम्भकर्णभूपति विजयराज्ये (Nagda Mewar epigraph of 1494/1437, *Prachin-Lekh Sangraha*, op.cit. I. 48).

15. R. V. Somani has made a mess of the inscriptions of the *JKS* and a review thereof is needed. He published its three inscriptions in the *Anekanta* Delhi, XXII-1 (April 1969) pp.37 ff. These had already been noticed in the *Annual Report on Indian Epigraphy (ARIE)* 1954-55, Srl No. 491 (from Udaipur Museum No. 8 six slabs) thus :—

"(It) records the setting up of a pillar (stambha) by
one Jiyā or Jījāka, son of Sānāya (Sā Nāya) of the
Sherawāla (Bagherawala) caste, cf. Bhandarkar List
No. 1852."

Obviously, these had already also been noticed by
Bhandarkar. Six rectangular pieces of the epigraph-stones
are preserved in the Victoria Hall Museum Udaipur, Regd.
at No. 13 (Handbook to the Victoria Hall Museum Udaipur,
Jaipur 1961, Srl No. 30, p.11). Somani's texts published
in the *Anekanta*, op.cit. and *Vir-Bhumi-Chittorgadh* (Jaipur
1969) pp.252, 265-68 were corrupt and full of
misreadings and gaps. These were corrected and reprinted
in the *Jaina-Śilālekha-Sangraha*, Vol. V (ed. V. Johrapurkar)
(Delhi 1971) pp.63-70 Srl Nos. 153-154-155. (Also see
references in G. N. Sharma's *Rajasthan-ke-Itihas-ke-Srota*
(Hindi) Vol. I (Jaipur 1973, pp.121-22).

An exactly similar Epigraph-stone is preserved in the
Udaipur Museum (cf. The Handbook, op.cit, p.11
Srl No. 31) Regd. at No. 24 being fragmentary, size 7 1/2"
X 6" recording the installation of a Jaina kīrttistambha at
Chittorgadh by Jījāka son of Sā (Sāh) Nāya of Bagherawala
caste.

Then, Somani claimed (vide his *History of Mewar*,
Jaipur 1976, p.92) that he found a new inscription which
proved that the *JKS* was built by the family of Jījā - his
father Nāya built Chandraprabha temle at Chittor - Jījā
began the *JKS* - it was completed by his son
Punyasingh-and the consecration ceremony was done by
Jaināchārya Dharmachandra of Mūlasaṅgh. This was not
discovered by Somani as it had already been noticed in
the *Annual Report of Indian Epigraphy* 1956-57, Srl No.
B-108, p.51 from a photograph in the National Museum,

being the photo of a fragment from Chittorgadh, obviously preserved there in the Topkhana Museum of the Central A.S.I.), thus:—

> "Dated in V. S. 1357 Phālguna su.......Sanskrit, Nagari, mentions Dharmachandra and his Guru-Parampara and appears to record the installation of a Māna-stambha."

The epigraph is written in 25 lines and contains 29 *Slokas*. It has also been quoted in the *Jaina-Śilālekha-Sangraha*, Vol. V, op.cit, pp.63-64 at Srl No. 152 and the fact that it had already been noticed in the *ARIE* 1956-57 at Srl. No. B-108 has also been attested. Somani's note (cf. *History of Mewar*, op.cit, p.92) that "on the basis of another unpublished inscription of 1357/1300, now lying in the office of the Central Archaeological Department Chittorgadh, it may be proved that it had been completed by them" refers to the same inscription and the knowledge of this epigraph-stone was never exclusive to him.

A very corrupt text of the Nandgaon (Karanja) image inscription, mentioning the *JKS*, dated in 1541/1484, was published by Agarchand Nahta: 'Chittor-ke-Jain-Kirttistambha-ka - Nirmana - kala evam Nirmata' *Anekanta* Delhi, Vol. VIII-3. This mentions:

मेदपाटदेशे चित्रकूटनगरे श्रीचन्द्रप्रभजिनेन्द्र-
चैत्यालयस्याग्रे निजभुजोपार्जित वित्तबलेन
श्री कीर्तिस्तम्भ: आरोपक साह जीजा (जीजाक)...

(Sāh Jījā or Jījāka who installed the Kīrttistambha in front of the Jaina temple of Çandraprabha at Chittorgadh by his own earned wealth). Somani also misquoted in *SP* XVI. 3-4 (July-Oct. 1965) pp.101-102 and misjoined it with the reference made in a different context in the Mahāvīra-Prāsāda-Praśasti of 1495/1438.

Somani borrowed the text of the 'Çitrakūta-Durga-Mahāvīra-Prāsāda-Praśasti' of 1495/1438 (which also mentioned the *JKS*) from the *Journal* of the Bombay Branch of the Royal Asiatic

Society, Vol. 23 (pp.42-60) wherein the full text along with an authoritative resume' of the epigraph was published by D. R. Bhandarkar. But Somani published it in a very corrupt form in his *Maharana Kumbha* (Hindi) (Jodhpur 1968) pp.372-84 and omitted a number of *ślokas,* including the vital ślokas Nos. 93 to 95, and also the colophon:—

इति श्रीचित्रकूटदुर्गमहावीरप्रासादप्रशस्तिश्च

चारुचक्रचूडामणिमहोपाध्याय श्री-

चारित्ररत्नगणिभिर्विरचिता ॥

संवत् १५०८ प्रजापतिसंवत्सरेदेवगिरौ महाराजधान्यामियं प्रशस्तिलेखि ॥

and he also did not mention the volume number of the journal from which he had taken it.

Then, in his article entitled: 'V. S. 1495-ki- Mahabira - Prasasti- ka-ek-Shilakhand' published in the *Varda* Bissau, XI-3 (July-Sept. 1968) 7-9, he claimed to have discovered a fragment of this inscription, bearing *ślokas* Nos. 91 to 104 and the colophon, being obviously the last piece of the slab, and published its text. But he did not collate it with Bhandarkar's text published in the *JBBRAS,* Vol. 23 and did not attempt to bring out a standard and authenticated text. Awful mistakes and gaps consequently remained. Thus his reading begins with *śloka* 91 which was Bhandarkar's 90. But latter's 91 was not there in his text. On the other hand his *ślokas* 92-93 were not there in Bhandarkar's text. Latter's 92 was given as 94 in his text. While serialisation of *ślokas* 95 to 104, more or less coincided, the most intriguing was the omission of Bhandarkar's ślokas 93-94 in Somani's text. In fact, these two *ślokas* were essential for the study of the *JKS.* These *ślokas* had also been omitted by Somani in his *Maharana Kumbha,* op.cit, p.383. As there he had borrowed his text from Bhandarkar's text where these were published, this omission could only be deliberate. What could be his intention to omit these two *ślokas* here is a matter of surmise, as he has already quoted them in the *SP* XVI. 3-4 (July-Oct. 1965) p.102. In any case, as the ms. copy from which Bhandarkar's text was published was made in 1508/1451, it is more reliable than Somani's patched text.

This is typical of Somani and he habitually plays with his data. He cited an inscription of V.S. 1041 (?) (cf. *Varda*, XIV-2, April-June 1971, pp.1-6) to prove that the Temple of Samādhīswara (which he erroneously calls 'Samiddheśwara') was built before Bhoja Paramāra (1018-54). But he did not reproduce text of such an important epigraph allegedly for administrative reasons. Nobody else has seen or used this inscription and if it was discovered by Somani there could not be any administrative reason preventing the publication of a vital evidence. This sounds intriguing. Veracity of Somani's statements in respect of inscriptions of Rajasthan have been often questioned, e. g. by Dasaratha Sharma, *Varda*, IX-4 (October 1966) p.32 apropos of Somani's article on an inscription of V.S. 1295, ibid, IX. 3 (July 1966) pp.4-6; and by B. L. Sharma, cf. *Varda* XVI-2 (April-June 1973) 51-52, apropos of Somani's article on Ghatiyala inscriptions, cf. Ibid XV-2 (April-June 1972) 4-7. He claims to have discovered many new inscriptions of Rajasthan which had already been noticed or published, for example in the : 1. Bhandarkar's List, 2. Bhavnagar Inscriptions, 3. Rajputana Museum Ajmer Reports, 4. Annual Reports of the Indian Epigraphy, 5. Annual Reports of the Archaeological Survey of India and its other publications, 6. Indian Antiquary, and other Indological journals prior to the Independence. Research is a strict discipline in itself and professional ethics demands the most precise referencing and documentation. He is also not authoritatively conversant with Sanskrit or Paleography and his readings are generally erroneous. His data has, therefore, to be used with greatest caution.

16. Cf. *ARIE* 1956-57, Srl No. B-108; *Jaina-Śilālekha-Sangraha (JSS)* Vol. V (ed. V. Johrapurkar) (Delhi 1971) Srl No. 152, p.63.

17. *Handbook* to the Victoria Hall Museum Udaipur (Jaipur 1961) p.11 Srl Nos. 30 and 31; Bhandarker's List No. 1852; *ARIE* 1954-55, Srl No. 491; *Jaina Śilālekha Sangraha*, Vol. V, Srl No. 154, p.68.

18. *JSS* Vol. V, op.cit, Srl No. 153, pp.65-67, given herewith under *Appendix* A (1).

19. *JSS*, Vol. V, op.cit, Srl No. 155, p.69-70.

20. D. R. Bhandarkar, 'Chittorgadh-Prasasti' *Journal of the Bombay Branch of the Royal Asiatic Society,* Vol. 23, op.cit, pp.42-60.

21. Text of the relevant verses 18-25 and 86-104 has been given herewith along with a translation in *Appendix* A (2).

22. Agarchand Nahta, cf. *Anekanta* Delhi VIII-3; its corrected and reconstructed text has been given herewith in *Appendix* A (3). For a geneological table of Jījāka as given in this inscription, see *Appendix* A (4). As this epigraph is mutilated at least four generations appear to be missing after Pūrṇasiṁha. Thus the 10th generation is mentioned in 1541/1484. Jījāka should have lived, therefore, in the 13th century and the date of the *JKS*, on the strength of this epigraph alone, can be fixed around 1300 A.D., as in fact, other epigraphs have unmistakably confirmed. Nahta's fixation of the date as c. 1500 A.D. on the basis of this geneology is not correct.

23. For these texts and translations see *Appendix* B (7).

24. *AP*, p.357.

25. Reference may be made in this connection to this author's paper: 'Minaret versus the Dhvajastambha' *Indica* Bombay VII-1 (March 1970) pp.19-31 and *History of Sultanate Architecture* (New Delhi 1978) pp.28-35.

26. Cf. this author's paper, op.cit.

27. For details, see *History of Sultanate Architecture*, op.cit, pp.20-35.

28. E.g. 'Mānastambha-mahāmidaṃ' (v.30) and 'Mānastambha-Pratiṣṭhāyā-mānam (v.45) of Pūrṇasiṁha-Praśasti of the *JKS* of c.1300 A.D. (cf. *Appendix* A (1)); verses 23, 86, 93, 94 etc of the Mahāvīra-Prāsāda-Praśasti of 1495/1438 (cf. *Appendix* A (2)); and

श्री चित्रकूटनगरे श्रीचन्द्रप्रभ जिनेन्द्रचैत्यालयस्याग्रे
निजभुजोपार्जित वित्तबलेन श्री कीर्तिस्तम्भ,

cf. the Karanja inscription of 1541/1484 (*Appendix* A (3).

29. Vide verse-86 of the Mahāvīra-Prāsāda-Praśasti.

30. Ibid, verse-92.

31. These monoliths have been discussed in details in chapters VI, VII and VIII of the author's impending work: *CHITTORGADH KIRTTISTAMBHA OF MAHARANA KUMBHA.* Also see *Appendix* B and C below.

32. This symbolism of *Trailokya* or *Jagat* in respect of the *JKS* has been discussed in details in the texts described below in *Appendix*-B.

33. *Viṣṇu-Dharmottara-Purāṇa* (abb. *VDP*), LXII, p.185.

34. Ibid, LXXV, p.206.

35. Ibid, LXXXIV, pp.220-21.

36. This has been discussed in chapters VI, VII and VIII of the author's above-cited monograph: *CHITTORGADH KIRTTISTAMBHA OF MAHARANA KUMBHA.*

37. It is likely that both Indian and Assyrian structures might have been derived from the same common source in a hoary past and they may be cognate to a common West Asiatic Culture.

* * *

APPENDICES

(A). EPIGRAPHS : TEXTS & TRANSLATIONS

1. Pūrṇasiṁha Praśasti of Jaina Kīrttistambha *(JKS)* (c. 1300 A.D.) (Text)
2. Citrakūṭa-Durga-Mahāvīra-Prāsāda-Praśasti of Guṇarāja (V.S. 1495/1438 A.D.) (Text & Translation)
3. Corrected and Reconstructed Inscription of V.S. 1541/1484 A.D. of Karanja (Nandgaon Image Inscription (Text)
4. Geneological Table of Jījāka as given in the Karanja (Nandgaon Image) Inscription of V.S. 1541/1484 A.D.

1. Pūrṇasiṁha-Prasasti of The JKS of Chittorgadh[1]
(C. 1300 A.D.)

सूनुस्तस्य तु दीनाको वाच्छ्रीभार्यासमन्वित:।

अध: सू (क) रोति पूजायै पुरंदरस(श) चीरुचम्॥ २१॥

नायाख्य: सूनुरस्यासीत् नायका (को) धर्मकर्मणि।

अथवा न---------- कर्मसु सर्द्ध (र्व) दा॥ २२॥

विशालकच्छकेतुच्छछायाछलध्वजव्रजै:।

निजप्रासादसौधाग्रनृत्यतुंगकरैरिव॥ २३॥

तत्र य: कारयामास ----------।

मंदिरं सुंदरं रप्यकाभ्यं सम्यक्त्ववे (चे) तसाम्॥ २४॥

स्व: सोपानोपदेशं द्रढयति च जिन: श्रीपदोत्कंठितानां

सोपानैर्मंडउपोपि प्रकटयति ह------ विवाह:।

उच्चै: प्रासादचंचत्कनकमयमहाकुंभशुंभद्ध्वाजाग्रै–

रारूढा नृत्यतीव प्रभुपदजयिनी मानसी सिद्धिरस्य॥ २५॥

नागश्रीसंगतो देन-------- जडाग्नय:।

कालकूटान्वयोन्माथी यो वृषांक: कलौ युगे॥ २६॥

हाल्लजिजुस्तथा न्योट्टलसमभिध: श्रीकुमारस्थिराख्य:

षष्ठ: श्रीए------पि विजयिनश्चक्रवर्ती श्रियस्तम्।

तेषां या (यो) जिजुनामाजनि जनिहनन प्राणापोराणमार्ग्य:

प्रज्ञातिश्रीत्रिवर्गप्रभुरमवदसौ जैन (धर्माभिलंबी)॥ २७॥

यश्चन्द्रप्रभमुच्चकूटघटनं श्री चित्रकूटे नटत्–

कोत्रत्पल्लवतालवीजनमरुप्रध्वस्तसुर्याश्रमे।

श्रीचैत्ये तलहट्टिका समवटी श्रीसादपीघ्या-------

1. Cf. 'Jaina-Silalekha-Sangraha' Vol. V (ed. V. Johrapurkar) (Bhartiya Jnana-Pitha, Delhi 1971) Srl No. 153, pp. 65-67; C. 1300 A.D.

------ वि जिनेश्वरस्य सदनं श्रीखोट्टरे सत्पुरे॥ २८॥

बूढाडीगरकेभघाच सुमिरौ जाने समारभ्य तनृ—

मानस्तंभमहादिमं ------ मिदं निर्वत्य ---- सत्यं स य

सुमंगलाय जयिने *श्रीपूर्णसिंहाय* वै।

गीर्वाणोदयिनीश्च यं समगम धर्मानुरागोल्वण:॥ ३०॥

पुण्यसिंहोपि धर्मधुराधवल वृंहण:।

जितारि: पितृसद्भारदत्तस्कंधो जयत्यसौ॥ ३१॥

किंचिदारोपितस्कंधोभ्यासयोगद्दिने दिने।

विषमेधिवलो भूयो धवल: शवलोचन:॥ ३२॥

अन्वयागतसद्धर्मभारधोरेयविक्रम:।

अकिणांकष्टशुस्कंध: पुण्यसिंहो महाद्भुतम्॥ ३३॥

यत्पुण्यं निटले भाति भारतीचक्रमंडले।

यत्कीर्तिस्त्रिजगत्सौधे धर्मलक्ष्मीर्मलांबुजे॥ ३४॥

अपूर्वोयं धनी कश्चिद् यच्छन्नपि यद्दच्छया।

वर्द्धयत्यनिशं स्वं स्वं परं सत्पुण्यसंचय:॥ ३५॥

उररीकृतनिर्वाहनिव सौम्यैव संपद:।

स्थिराश्रयपदं भेजुस्तेजोकृभित्तविग्रहा:॥ ३६॥

पुण्यसिंहो जयत्येष दानिनां जनकुंजर:॥

यत्कीर्तिकामिनीनेत्रे कज्जलं भुवनांबरम्॥ ३७॥

किं मेरु: कनकप्रभ: किमु हरिर्गिर्वाण ----- प्रिय:

किं सोम: सकलं चकार ------- पुण्योदयात्।

पेयं धर्मधुराधरा (रो) विजयते श्रीपूर्णसिंह: कलौ॥ ३८॥

किं मेरु: किं न मेरु: किमुत सुरगुरु: किं हरि: किं मुरारि:

किं रुद्र: किं समुद्र: किमुत च विलसच्चंद्रिकाचन्द्रचंद्र:।

उन्नव्या स्वेष्टदत्या विमलतरधियासद्धि भूत्या विमत्या

गोनीत्या रत्नभृत्या सकलतनुतयापूर्णसिंह: पृथिव्याम्॥ ३९॥

ध्येयस्तस्य विशालकीर्तिमुनिप: सारस्वतश्रीलता—

कंदोद्भेदधनायमानवधन: स्याद्वाद विद्यापति:।

वर्गत्यासगर्वचोविलोमविलसदृंभोलिदीर्यत्यस

क्षोणीच्चतमयास्तपोनिधिसावासीद्धरित्रीतले॥ ४०॥

कताकार्कार्छ(र्क)श्यं कृसित परवादिद्दिपमदं

क्व नि: श्रीमत्प्रेमप्रचुररसनिस्यंदिकविता।

उपन्यासप्राप्ते क्व च विहितवर्गव्यजनिता
मनोगम्यं रम्यं श्रुतमिह यदीयं विलसितम्॥ ४१ ॥
योगानंगत्रिनेत्रस्त्रिभुवनरचनानूतनेपि त्रिनेत्रो
मीमांसावाग्निरोधप्रकटनदिनकृत् सांख्यमत्तेभसिंह: ।
उद्घद्वोद्वाहिदर्पस्फुरदुजगरूड: प्रौढयाधीकशैल–
श्रेणीसंपातशंपाकलितवरवचोवर्णिनीवल्लभो य: ॥ ४२ ॥
तत्पुत्र: शुभकीर्तिरुर्जिततपोनुष्ठाननिष्ठापति:
श्रीसंसारविकारकारणगुणस्तृप्यन्मनोदेवत: ।
प्रारब्धाय पदप्रयाणकलसत्पंचाक्षरोन्वारण–
पुत्यत्कीकृत निर्भवे हिमककृक्षबधत्समाध्याब्धिठ: ॥ ४३ ॥
सिद्धांतोदधिवीचिवद्धनस्त्रद्धंद्रोवितंद्रोधुना
विख्यातोस्ति समग्रशुद्धचरित: श्रीधर्मेव– – – – – – यति: ।
तत्कीर्ति: किल धीरवार्द्धिनृपतिश्रीनारसिंहादिह
स्वीकृत्य प्रकटीचकार सततं हमीरवीरोप्यसौ ॥ ४४ ॥
तच्चरणकमलमधुपे मानस्तंभप्रतिष्ठया मानम्।
प्रकटीचकार भुवने धनिक: श्रीपूर्णसिंहोत्र॥ ४५ ॥

2. Çitrakūṭa-Durga-Mahāvīra-Prāsāda- Praśasti of Guṇarāja [1] (V. S. 1495/1438 A.D.)

TEXT :

तस्याङ्गजो जगदगञ्जितदिव्यतेजा: श्रीमान्नवार्क इव राजति कुम्भकर्ण: ।
दिव्यस्य य: क्षितिभृतां शिरसि स्वपादन्दूरास्तदुर्णयतमा भुवनं पुनाति ॥ १८ ॥
लाट: स्विद्यल्लालाट: कटरटनपटु: भोटभूप: प्रदाता,
कर्णाट पू:कपाटंमुखपुट घटितस्वाङ्गुलिर्जङ्गलेन्द्र: ॥
नश्यद्वङ्ग: कलिङ्ग: कुरुरुरुविनयो मालव: कालवक्त्र–
स्त्यक्तौजा गूजरीन्द्र: समजनि जयिनस्तस्य राज्ञ: प्रवाणे ॥ १९ ॥
उच्छेत्तुं कमलं न कण्टककमलं मित्रोपकारादपि,
स्वस्यापीति ततोऽपसृत्य कमला निष्कण्टकां मेदिनीम् ॥
कुर्वाणं स्वयमेव पाणिकमलं शिश्राय यस्वानिशं
नम्रानेकमहीपति: स जयति श्रीकुम्भपृथ्वीपति: ॥ २० ॥
अस्त्यद्भुत: क्षितिधर: किल चित्रकूटस्तेनावनीमघवता परिपाल्यमान: ॥
श्रीमेदपाटधरणीतरुणीललाटपट्टे स्फुटं मुकुटतामुपटीकते य: ॥ २१ ॥
नानाविकस्वरसिताम्बुजराजितानि
राजन्ति निर्मलपयांसि सरांसि यत्र ॥
जाने यदुन्नतविहारविदीर्णमूर्ते–
व्योमनश्युतानि शकलानि सतारकाणि ॥ २२ ॥
तीर्थाधारतयारिदुर्मतयोन्नत्याद्भुतेत्वेन वा,
स्पर्धां भो विदधाति य: सहमया सद्द्य: समायातु स: ।

---

1. Cf. *Journal* of the Bombay Branch of the Royal Asiatic Society Bombay, Vol. 23, pp. 42-60 (D. R. Bhandarkar's article : 'Çitrakūṭa - Durga - Mahāvīra - Prāsada - Praśasti' based on Ms. No. 1332 of Prof. Kathavate's report for the years 1891-95) ślokas 18-25 and 86-104. The Praśasti was composed in V.S. 1495/1438 A.D. and this copy made in 1508/1451.

इत्याकारयतीव निर्झररवैरुर्वीधरान्य: परा–
न्कीर्तिस्तम्भमिषेण हस्तमतनुं प्रोत्तभ्यवादोन्मना: ॥ २३ ॥
व्योमाङ्गणादनवलम्बनिवासजात–
स्वेदेव देवनगरी यदुपत्यकायाम् ॥
चक्रेऽवत ------ मवनौ नगरछलेन
निश्रेणिदन्डमिव यं गिरिमाकलय्य ॥ २४ ॥
वार्तापि तापविषयात्र कथं प्रजानां
श्रीकुम्भकर्णपृथिवीपति--- ----- द्भुतौजा: ॥
छित्वा यत: क्षितिभृतामभितोऽपि वंशा–
नेकातपत्रमयमत्र तनोति राज्यम् ॥ २५ ॥

------------- ----

उच्चैर्मण्डपपङ्क्तिदेवकुलिकाविस्तीर्यमाणश्रियं,
कीर्तिस्तम्भसमीपवर्तिनममुं श्रीचित्रकूटाचले ॥
प्रासादं सृजत: प्रसादमसमं श्रीमोकलोर्वीपते–
रादेशाद्गुणराजसाधुरमितस्वर्दृघ्योदधार्षीन्मुदा ॥ ८६ ॥
नानान्तरायतिमिराणि निहन्तुमत्र
यस्योद्यमस्तरुणतिग्ममरांचकार ॥
बालाभिधोऽस्य तनय: सनयश्चिरायु–
रस्तु प्रशस्तगुणसंपदकम्पकीर्ति: ॥ ८७ ॥
नेत्राणाममृताञ्जनं त्रिजगत: श्रीचित्रकूटाचला–
लङ्कार: सविहार उज्ज्वलवपुर्विभ्राजतेऽभ्रंलिह: ॥
जाने श्रीगुणराजसाधुयशसां विश्वेऽप्यमातामयं
पिण्डीभूय महोच्छ्रय: समुदय: स्थेमानमास्तिघ्नुते ॥ ८८ ॥
अस्य त्रिलोकैकविलोकनीयां सौन्दर्यलक्ष्मीमवलोकमान: ।
व्याक्षिप्तचेता इव सप्तसप्तिर्मध्यं दिने याति विलम्बमान: ॥ ८९ ॥
मूर्तोऽयं किमु *सोमसुन्दरगुरो:* पुण्योपदेशोच्चय:
प्राप्तो वा *गुणराजसाधुसुकृतस्तोम:* किमध्यक्षताम् ।
पिण्डीकृत्य सुधारस: सुकृतिनां टङ्कपारणेवोन्नत–
स्थानेऽस्थापि जगत्कृतेतिकृतिभिर्नो तर्क्यते कैरयम् ॥ ९० ॥
तत्र श्रीजिनशासनोन्नतिकरैरत्यद्भुतैरुत्सवै–
र्नव्यां श्रीवर*सोमसुन्दरगुरुप्रष्ठै*: प्रतिष्ठापिताम् ॥

वर्षे श्रीगुणराजसाधुतनयाः पञ्चाष्टरत्नप्रभे

न्यास्थन्त प्रतिमामिमामनुपमां श्रीवर्धमानप्रभोः॥ ९१ ॥

शोभावन्ध्यः स विन्ध्यः सुरगुरु ------ नोच्चकूटस्त्रिकूटः

कैलासश्चाविलासो हिमगिरिरमहान्वामनाभः सुनाभः ।

मैनाकः पाकरूपः सकलवसुमतीदत्तनेत्रप्रसादे

प्रासादे द्योतमाने रविरथतुरगप्राप्तविश्रान्तिकेऽस्मिन्॥ ९२ ॥

रागद्वेषजितो जिनस्य विजयस्तम्भौ किमुत्तम्भितौ

पारावारदुरन्तदुर्गतियुगोत्ताराय सेतू किमु ।

किं वोच्चैस्त्रिदिवापवर्गगमने निश्रेणिदण्डाविमौ

कीर्तिस्तम्भममुं च वीक्ष्य विदधत्येवं विकल्पान्न के॥ ९३ ॥

सोपानपद्धतिभिमामधिरूढ़ा भव्याः

स्वर्गापवर्गभवनेषु सुखं रमध्वम्॥

इत्येष वक्ति किल हस्तमुदस्य

कीर्तिस्तम्भच्छलेन निनदैरिव किङ्किणीनाम्॥ ९४ ॥

प्राग्वंशस्य ललाम मण्डपगिरिं शोभां नयन्त्रैष्टिक-

प्रष्ठः प्रत्यहमष्टधा जिनपते पूजाः सृजन् द्वादश॥

सङ्घाधीशकुमारपालसुकृती कैलासलक्ष्मीहृती

दक्षं दक्षिणतोऽस्य सोदरमिव प्रासादमादीधपत्॥ ९५ ॥

ऊकेशवंशतिलकः सुकृतोरुतेजा-

स्तेजात्मज प्रतिवसन्निह चित्रकूटे॥

चाचाह्वयः सुजनलोचनदत्तशैत्यं

चैत्यं च चारु निरमीमपदुत्तरस्याम्॥ ९६ ॥

सर्वत्रागुञ्जिता कीर्तिर्गुणराजस्य गर्जतु॥

येन श्रीधर्मसाम्राज्यमसृज्यत कलौ युगे॥ ९७ ॥

यः कल्लोलवतीपतेः कलयितुं कल्लोलमालां प्रभु-

र्निष्णातश्च नभोगणे गणयितुं यस्तारकाणांगणम्॥

यो मातुं सिकताकणांश्च सरितां शक्तः स एव ध्रुवं

संख्यातुं गुणराजसाधुविहितश्रीधर्मकार्याण्वलम्॥ ९८ ॥

तेजस्विनो विजयिनो गुणराजसुता जयन्तु चिरमेते।

श्रीजिनशासनसौधे स्तम्भा इव ये विभासन्ते॥ ९९ ॥

यद्विद्यानां विनेया यदुरुगुणनुतेराननान्युतमानां

श्राद्धा यद्बोधशक्तेः सकलवसुमती यद्यशोमण्डलस्य॥

ब्राह्मी यत्रौढिमोक्तेर्गुरुरपि मरुतां तत्त्ववादस्य येषां
यद्बुद्धेर्बोध्यभावां न हि विषयतया यान्ति पर्याप्तियोगम् ॥ १०० ॥
शिष्य: प्रशस्तिमेतां तेषां श्रीसोमसुन्दरगुरुणाम् ।
शरनिधिमनु (१४९५) मितवर्षे चक्रचारित्ररत्नगणि: ॥ १०१ ॥
लक्षस्य सूत्रदक्षस्य नन्दनो नारद: प्रशस्तिमिमाम् ॥
उत्कीर्णवान्सुवर्णां लिखितां संवेगजयतिना ॥ १०२ ॥
श्रीचित्रकूटाचलत्मौलिमौलिरमोधितोर्वीजनदृष्टिसृष्टि: ॥
देयादमेया: शरद: प्रमोदं सतां *महावीरविहारराज:* ॥ १०३ ॥
यावल्लीलां विधत्ते सततमुदयिभिर्दीपितेज: प्रतानै—
युक्ता मुक्तावलीयं हृदि विशदगुण सिद्धिलक्ष्मीस्मिताख्या: ॥
प्रासादस्तावदेषोऽभ्युदयतु विदुषां हर्षमेषां प्रशस्ति—
र्दत्तां धत्तां नितान्तं जिनमतमदयं प्रीयतां सर्वलोक: ॥ १०४ ॥
   इति श्रीचित्रकूटदुर्गमहावीरप्रासादप्रशस्तिश्चचारुचक्रचूडामणिमहोपाध्यायश्री—
   चारित्ररत्नगणिभिर्विरचिता ॥
संवत् १५०८ प्रजापतिसंवत्सरे देवगिरी महाराजधान्यामियं प्रशस्तिलेखि ॥

TRANSLATION

King Mokala was succeeded by his son Kumbhakarna (Kumbha) who illumined the world like (a new) Sun and ruled over the earth in a divine way (18). He conquered Lāṭa, Bhoṭa, Karṇāṭa, Jāṅgala, Kaliṅga, Kuru, Mālava and Gurjara countries (19). He rendered the Earth fearless and pleased it like Lotus flower (This is purely eulogical) (20). The wonderful mountain Citrakūṭa (Chittorgadh) which crowns the Medapāṭa country as 'mukuṭa' crowns a young lady, is guarded by Him (21). Chittorgadh is adorned by many tanks which have crystal clear water and white lotus of several varieties in full bloom. These dazzling water-sheets look like pieces of the Sky with stars, torn asunder due to excessive merriment of gods (22). Chittorgadh is full of many tīrthas, it is difficult to approach, it is very high and it is wonderful. These are its four unique features. It seems that it is challenging other mountains to come and try to compete with it. It has rippling water-falls and the Kīrttistambha (viz. the *JKS*) in which matters too it is unexcelled (23). Town of the gods which had no support descended from heaven to the earth through this mountain as a ladder and settled as Nagara (Nagari near Chittorgadh) at its foot (24). Here ruled Kumbha, Lord of the Earth with justice and care of his subjects (This is eulogical verse) (25)..........................

Chittorgadh is adorned with rows of high maṇḍapas and beautiful spacious temples. Here, at the behest of the King Mokal who conferred unequal favours on him, the saintly Guṇarāja re-built the temple (of Mahāvīra) near the Kīrttistambha (viz. the *JKS*) for the restoration of Dharma (86). He exerted like the Sun at zenith for the mitigation of darkness. His son Bāla supervised the construction work. May he live long and his fame remain for ever (87). This temple of Mahāvīra which Guṇarāja rebuilt looked pleasant to the eyes. It is an ornament of Chittorgadh which is unique in the three worlds. It has a Vihāra. It is beautiful and very high. It seems that the fame of Guṇarāja which this world is not able to contain, has been personified in the form of this temple (88). The Sun is delayed on his journey to the zenith because he is absorbed in looking at the beauty of this temple at Chittorgadh which is unique and worth-seeing in the three worlds (89). This temple is either a deified form of the sacred teachings of Somasundara (Guru of Guṇarāja); or it is personification of the good deeds (Puṇya) of Guṇarāja; or it is the nectar of the meritorious people for the ritualistic dedication of the eye-that is why the Creator has established it on such a high place. So argue the wise (90). The son of the Saint Guṇarāja had the new image of Vardhamāna (Mahāvīra, 24th Tīrthankara) placed here in V.S. 1485/1428 A.D. for the propagation of Jainism and the consecration ceremonies were performed by Guru Somasundara.

(This shows that Guṇarāja began the reconstruction of the Mahāvīra temple but he did not live to see its completion and the image was installed by his son) (91). In comparison to this beautiful temple of Vardhamāna which is pleasing to the eyes of the people of the whole world, the Vindhyā Mountain has become lustreless; Trikūṭa has no high śikharas; The Himālaya and Kailāśa have lost their charm; Sunābha has become smaller and Maināka has been reduced to a mediocre size. It is so high and beautiful. On its rest the horses of the Chariot of the Sun at zenith (92). On perceiving this temple of Mahāvīra (built by Guṇarāja) and the Kīrttistambha (viz. the *JKS*) adjoining it, everybody began to surmise that these towers of Victory were raised in honour of the Jina who had triumphed over worldly attachment and hatred; or these were two bridges for crossing the boundless ocean; or these are stairs of the ladder to go to the Heaven (Apavarga, Nirvāṇa). The people who look at the Kīrttistambha (viz. the *JKS*) so surmise (93). 'O Pious People, ascend its stairway, reach the Heaven and live in the gorgeous Heavenly Tabernacle with perpetual Bliss' - Chittorgadh is proclaiming this through the sound of its bells and by raising its hand in the form of this Kīrttistambha (the *JKS*) (94). Verses 95 and 96 are important as they describe the situation of two other temples in its vicinity. The first one was built to the south of the Mahāvīra temple of Guṇarāja by one Kumārapāla of the Prāgvaṁśa (Porwal family) who was also the Sanghādhīśa. This temple was extremely beautiful and in it regular arrangement was made for the 12 kinds of worship of the Jinas, eight times a day (95). To its north was an elegant Ċaitya (Jaina temple) which was built by one Chacha, son of Teja, of Ukeśa-vaṁśa (Oswal family). He was a man of good deeds and he built it for the benefit of the people (96). The following four verses in praise of Guṇarāja, are purely eulogical. The fame of Guṇarāja and his meritorious religious deeds is resounding everywhere. He has established a Dharma-Rājya in the Kaliyuga (97). He is like sea in which rivers flow in. Similarly he has stored good deeds. He has secured for himself a specific place among the terrestrial bodies like Dhruva (98). May the able sons of Guṇarāja live long. They are adornments of Jainism like pillars of this temple (99). Inspite of the fact that the sons of Guṇarāja are unexcelled in Vidyās and other attainments, they are modest. Their fame is spreading in the whole world (100). This praśasti was composed by Cāritra-Ratna-Gaṇi, who was pupil of Śrī Somasundara, in the year V.S. 1495 (101). It was written (i.e. calligraphed) by a jati named Samvegaja and engraved by Nārada, son of the Sūtradhāra Lakṣa (Lakha) (102). May this great temple of Mahāvīra adorn Chittorgadh and please the eyes of the people for ever and ever (103). As long as this world remains, the beauty and glory of this temple will illuminate the world and this praśasti will please the learned people. May Jainism prosper (104).

And thus ends the praśasti of the Mahāvīra temple situated at Chittorgadh. It has been composed by the learned Cāritra-Ratna-Gaṇi. It was copied in the Prajāpati year 1508 at Devagiri during the reign of Maharaja Dhānya (Colophon).

3. Corrected and Reconstructed Inscription of V.S. 1541/1484 A.D. of Karanja.

स्वस्ति श्री संवत् १५४१ वर्षे शाके — प्रवर्त्तमाने — संवत्सरे — मासे शुक्ल पक्षे ६ दिने शुक्रवासरे स्वातिनक्षत्रे योगे २ करणे मिथुन लग्ने श्री वैराट देशे कारंजानगरे श्री श्री सुपार्श्वनाथ चैत्यालयो श्री मूलसंघे सेनगणे पुष्करगच्छे श्रीमन् वृद्धसेनगणधराचार्ये पारंपर्यादगत श्री देववीर महावादवादीश्वर रायवादियिकी महासकल विद्वज्जन् सार्व्वभौम साभिमानवादीमसिंहभिनवत्रै ------- विद्यसोमसेन भट्टारकाणामुपदेशात् श्री बघेरवालजातीय खमड़वाड़ गोत्रे अष्टोत्तरशत् महोत्तुंगशिखरप्रासाद समुद्धरणो धीरः त्रिलोक श्री जिनमहाभिबौद्धारक अष्टोत्तरशत् श्री जिनमहाप्रतिष्ठाकारक अष्टादशस्थाने अष्टादशकोटिश्रुत भण्डार संस्थापक सपादलक्षबंदीमोक्षकारक मेदपाटदेशे चित्रकूटनगरे श्री चन्द्रप्रभ जिनेन्द्रचैत्यालयस्याग्रे निजभुजोपार्जितवित्तबलेन श्री कीर्तिस्तम्भ आरोपक साह जीजा (जीजाक) सुत साह पूनसिंहस्य (पूर्णसिंहस्य) -------- साह देउ (देव = देवसिंह) तस्य भार्या वूह (?) तुकाइ तयोः पुत्र चत्वरः (चतुरसिंह) तेषु प्रथम पुत्र साह लखमण (लक्ष्मण) भार्या जसमाई सुत संघवी हंसराज भार्या हाराई द्वितीय पुत्र सा. भीम तृतीय पुत्र संघवी वीरन (वीरसिंह) भार्या संघविणि गौराइ ------- चतुर्थ पुत्र — मदे (?) भार्या पदमाई तयोः सुताः मं. पूनसी (पूर्णसिंह) सा. धर्मसी (धर्मसिंह) सा. देवसी (देवसिंह) ------- चैत्यालयोद्धरणधीरेण निजभुजोपार्जितवित्तानुसारेण महायात्रा प्रतिष्ठा तीर्थक्षेत्र -----

4. Geneological Table of Jījāka as given in the Inscription of V. S. 1541/1484 A.D.

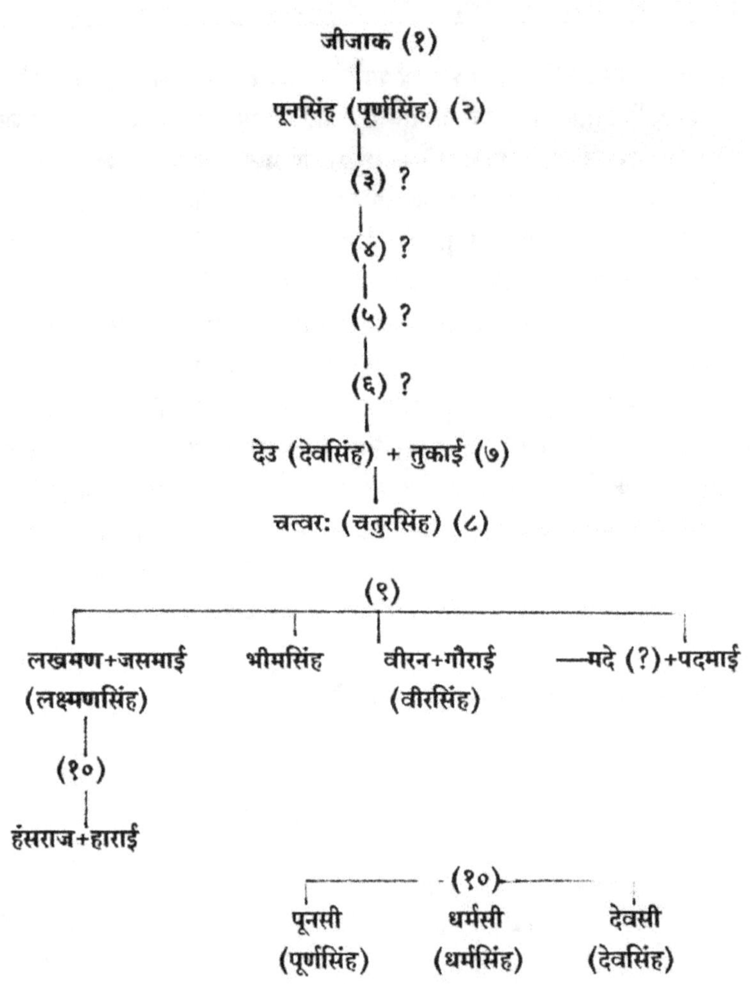

APPENDICES

(B). SANSKRIT TEXTS, COMMENTARIES & TRANSLATIONS

1. *Tiloya-Paṇṇati* (Trailokya-Prajnapti) (c. 9th century A.D.) on Cosmic Architecture

2. *Dīpārṇava, Jina-Darśana* and *Śilpa-Smriti- Vāstuvidyāyāṃ* (15th century A.D.) Texts on Parikara, Samavasaraṇa, Aṣṭāpada, Merugiri and Nandīśvara-Dwīpa

3. Texts on the worship of Meru, Nandīśvara-Dwīpa and Aṣṭāpada

4. *Viṣṇu-Dharmottara-Purāṇa* (III Khaṇḍa) (c. 7th century A.D.) Text on Ākāśa (Gagana), Vyoman and Aiḍūka

5. *Māna-Stambha-Pūjā* (Ms.)

6. *Stūpa-Lakṣaṇa-Kārikā-Vivaiçanaṃ* (Ms.)

7. *Aparājitapṛcchā* (late 12th century A.D.) on Kīrttistambha (Texts and Translations)

8. *Vāstu-Vidyā* (c. 15th century A.D.) on Kīrttistambha (Text and Translation)

9. *Dīpārṇava* (c. 15th century A.D.) on Kīrttistambha (Text and Translation)

10. *Vividha-Tīrtha-Kalpa* and other Texts on Aṣṭāpada, Nandīśvara-Dwīpa and Samavasaraṇa

1. *TILOYA-PANNATI* (Trailokya-Prajñapti) of Vṛṣabhācārya (Prakrit) (ed. by. A. N. Upadhyaye & H. L. Jain) (tr. in Hindi by Balchand Sastri in 3 vols, Sholapur).

According to Phoolchandra ('Vartamān Tiloya-Pannati aur uske rachñakāl ādi kā vichār' *Jaina Siddhant Bhaskar* Arrah, XI. 1, June 1944, pp. 65-82), it was originally authored by Āçārya Yati Vṛṣabha between 450 and 600 after the nirvāṇa of Mahāvīra. Its present recension was made between 738 and 900 Śaka (= 9th — 10th century A.D.) by Āçārya Jinasena. It is a Jaina Digambar work thus of great antiquity, comprised of 8000 ślokas in Prakrit Gāthā (poetry), parts also being in prose. It deals with various subjects related to Jaina concept of the Universe as Nāma, Sthāpanā, Drvya, Ksetra, Kāla and Bhāva, its square and cubic area, Vṛttāsana, Yavamadhya, Girikaṭaka, Dūṣya, and other forms with astonishingly precise mathematical calculations. Its 3rd chapter deals with 'Bhawana' or **Cosmic Architecture.** Architectural subjects have also been dealt with in the 4th chapter : 'Manuṣya-Loka'. Its chapters are as follows :

1. Sāmānya Loka
2. Nāraka Loka
3. Bhawanawāsī Loka
4. Manuṣya Loka
5. Tiryañça Loka
6. Vyantara Loka
7. Jyotiṣī Loka
8. Kalpawāsī Loka
9. Siddha Loka

Vihāra, stūpa, sabhā-bhawana, gandhakuṭī, vedikā etc are made for the Tīrthankaras. Altogether, they are called Samavasaraṇa which is a predecessor of Jaina temples and çaityālayas. Samavasaraṇa of Tīrthankaras combine stūpa, stambha, caitya-vṛksa, citrapaṭa, dharma-cakra etc. and it is described in the *Tiloya-Paṇṇati in details.*

2. *DĪPĀRṆAVA* (Sanskrit text edited with Gujarati tr. by P.O. Sompura, Palitana 1960): It is a North Indian Vāstu text of the Viśwakarmān school of c. 15th century A.D. Its second half portion (Uttarārdha) entitled *Jina-Darśana* is devoted to Jaina Art and Architecture (pp. 309-488). It prescribes the construction of four basic structures of Jaina sacred architecture viz. Parikara, Samavasaraṇa Aṣṭāpada and Nandīśvara-Dwīpa in details:

Chapter 22. Jina Parikara Lakṣaṇa   pp. 366-383
Chapter 25. Śrī-Samavasaraṇa   pp. 446-458
Chapter 26. Aṣṭāpada-Svarūpa   pp. 459-466
Chapter 27. Merugiri-Svarūpaṃ
   and Nandīśvara-Dwīpa Raçanā   pp. 467-472

Jina-Darśana part of the *Dīpārṇava* has also been published separately under the title: *Dīpārṇava-Jinadarśana* (Sanskrit text edited with Gujarati tr. by P. O. Sompura, Palitana 1960). Chapters 22, 25, 26 and 27 on Parikara, Samavasaraṇa, Aṣṭāpada and Nandīśvara-Dwīpa have been reproduced vide pp. 58-75, 138-150, 151-158 and 159-164 respectively. A detailed Introduction and an additional Appendix on Caitya, Stūpa, Vihāra and Stambha (viz. Kīrttistambha) have also been added to this work. The matter on Samavasaraṇa, Aṣṭāpada and Nandīśvara-Dwīpa has also been reprinted, ad-verbatim, in the 10th chapter entitled: 'Jina-Kalpadruma' of the work: *Śilpa-Smṛit-Vāstuvidyāyāṃ* (Uttarārdha) (edited with Gujarati tr. by N. C. Sompura, Palitana 1979) (vide pp. 465-475, 475-481 and 482-485 respectively).

They have been described in these works as follows:

(A) **'Parikara'** *(Fig. 10)* has been described, in 50 ślokas, as a beautiful architecture, for seating the image of the main Jina

Tīrthankara within the forum of the temple, in such distinct parts as 'siṁhāsana', 'cāmaradharā' and 'chatravṛta-daulā' with several rathikās and toraṇas. Along with divine symbols, it also contains paraphernalia of Royalty as siṁhāsana, cāmara, chatra, daṇḍa, tilaka, daulā and :

झल्लरी मणिमौक्तिकस्योर्ध्वे कलशशोभितम् ।[1]

How the Vītarāga-Jina could be associated with these insignia of sovereignty is an interesting question. Was it simply an architectural need ?

(B) **'Samavasaraṇa'** *(Fig. 11)* is made by the gods on the nirvāṇa of the Jina. It is sarvatobhadra (four-faced = visible on all the four sides). Three traditional mouldings : gajathara, aśvathara and narathara must be made on the bhiṭṭ of its mahāpīṭha :

पीठबन्धं   प्रकर्तव्यं   भिट्टत्रयसमन्वितम् ॥
महापीठं   प्रकर्तव्यं   गजाश्वं   च   नरादिकम् ॥

It has jagati, pīṭha, prākāra, maṇḍovara, maṇḍapa (and other traditional parts of the Hindu temple) and is crowned by Meru śikhara. It also has a 'parikara' with illikā-toraṇa and siṁhāsana :

इल्लिका तोरणैर्युक्तं परिकरं सिंहासनं ।

It is built in the **Merucchanda**. Gods and goddesses are despicted in accordance with their respective positions which are duly prescribed. Thus it is not an architectural accessory only, but a perfect architecture in itself, independent and unitary. As it was built by the gods on the nirvāṇa of the Jina, it is essentially a **funereal** memorial which was given a form to **commemorate** the Jina. Gradually, it assumed a **votive** character and came into worship, as it seems, much prior to a temple-form coming into being in the centuries before Christ. Later, when temple became a religious shrine, its form was retained and its votive significance continued.

---

1. Its form and iconography have been discussed in the 15th century work of Iconography, The *Rūpa-Maṇḍana* (ed. and tr. Balram Srivastava, Varanasi V. S. 2021) pp. 212-13, Chapter-VI, ślokas 33-39.

(C) **'Aṣṭāpada'**[1], *(Fig. 12)* like samavasaraṇa, is associated with the nirvāṇa of the Jina. King Bharata built the first aṣṭāpada on the place where the first Tīrthankara Ṛṣabhadeva was cremated and this too was, thus, originally a **commemorative funereal** structure, which later became votive. While samavasaraṇa can be both circular (vṛttākāra) and square (caturāsra), Aṣṭāpada is a miniature square and eight-terraced temple having doors on all the four sides:

भूमिश्चभूमिमानेन चतुर्द्वारयुतं शुभम्।

It has karṇikās, bhadras, vedikās, āsanapaṭṭikās, illikā-toraṇa and mahāmeru-śikhara with śṛṅgas, uruḥ-śṛṅgas and aṇḍaka-kalaśa. It is auspicious and its worship has been prescribed for happiness and prosperity:

तस्मात्सर्वं प्रयत्नेन कर्तव्यं च पूजागम:।

तत्कृतं च शुभं ज्ञेयं सर्वकामफलप्रदम्॥

पुत्र पौत्र प्रबर्द्धन्ते प्रजाराज्ञजयवहम्॥

(D) **Meru-Giri** and **Nandīśvara-Dwīpa**: *(Figs. 13-14)* Meru-giri, a representation of the mythological 'Meru' or 'Sumeru' is circular (vṛttākāra) which is made in three terraces named Nandana-Vana, Somanasa-Vana, and Paṇḍaka-Vana,[2] above which is Cūlikā on which rests the Jina-Caitya. It contains the siddha-śilā on which was born the Jina and this structure is thus made to celebrate the birth-place of the Jina: जन्माभिषेकस्तत्र च। Miniature temples dedicated to the Jinas and step-wells are built on the terraces and living creatures are faithfully depicted.

Nandīśvara-Dwīpa is representation of mythological mountain with 52 summits (kūṭas), each having a four-faced, four-doored, caitya. Subsidiary mountains and summits are duly

---

1. Samavasaraṇa and Aṣṭāpada have been dealt with in the *Prāsāda-Mañjarī* of Nātha (ed. P.O. Sompura, Ahmedabad, 1965) in the chapter on 'Jina-Prāsāda-Raçanā' pp. 1-24.

2. *Viṣṇu-Dharmottara-Purāṇa*, Third Khaṇḍa (ed. Priyabala Shah, Baroda 1958) Chapter-75: 'Vyoman', p. 206, designates them 'Bhadrapīṭhās.

made on all sides. Each çaitya has four images of jinas, there thus being 208 images in all. This is also an **architecture** prescribed for a **votive** purpose.

3. Such works as *PAÑCA-MERU-NANDĪSVARA* and *NANDĪSVARA-DWĪPA-BRHAT-VIDHĀNA* mention: नन्दीश्वरद्वीपे चतुर्दिक्षु द्वापञ्चाशत्जिनालयानि and prescribe rituals for their worship. Texts as *Sanskrit-Praçīna - Stavana - Sandohaḥ* (ed. Muni Vishalvijay, Ujjain V.S. 1995) mention: द्वीपे नन्दीश्वरे मेरुनगेषु रुचकादिषु (p. 42) and eulogize the sacredness of the **Aṣṭāpada** (p. 47) as follows:

अष्टापदनगोत्तंसान्   वृषभादिजिनेश्वरान्।
मानवर्णजुषो वन्दे चतुर्विंशंतिमादरात्॥ १ ॥
अहो भाग्यमहो पुण्यं तेषामद्भुतमङ्गिनाम्।
येषामष्टापदे देवान् नन्तुं शक्ति: पटीयसी॥ २ ॥
धन्योऽसौ भरतश्चक्री सौवर्णं जिनमन्दिरम्।
गिरावष्टापदे येन कारितं प्रतिमान्वितम्॥ ३ ॥
इहस्था अपि ये तत्र धृत्वा चित्ते जिनोत्तमान्।
वन्दन्ते सर्वदा तेषां मुक्तिश्रीर्वंशवर्त्तिनी॥ ४ ॥
एवं भक्त्या स्तुता महां जिनेन्द्रा ऋषभादय:।
बोधिलाभं प्रयच्छन्तु संसारे तिष्ठते सदा॥ ५ ॥

4. The Third Khaṇḍa of the *VIṢṆU-DHARMOTTARA-PURĀṆA* (middle of the 7th century A. D.) (ed. by Priyabala Shah, Vol. I: Text, G. O. S. No. 130, Oriental Institute Baroda 1958; English rendering Vol. II, G. O. S. No. 137, Baroda 1961) (abb. *VDP*) is one of the basic and earliest texts on Fine Arts, dealing with Gīta (Music), Nṛtta (Dance), Çitra (Painting), Pratimā (Iconography) and Prāsāda (Temple Architecture). The Sūtra on Iconography contains 42 chapters and is, by far, the most extensive. In its chapter 62 (Vol. I, p. 185) it prescribes the rūpa (form) of Ākāśa (or Ġagana) as a personified deity with two hands having Sun and Moon. It has thus been prescribed as a **Sculpture.** But in

Chapter-75 (Vol. I, p. 206, Vol. II pp. 153-54) 'Vyoman' (which is though a synonym of 'Ākāśa' and 'Gagana') is described as an **Architecture.** It is made in the from of Meru. It is quadrangular at the base and assumes a circular form above. Again it is quadrangular at the top. This part is called 'Bhadrapīṭha'. It has columns. On it is another 'Bhadrapīṭha' on which an eight-petalled lotus is placed. In the middle of the pericarp, on the petals, is placed the **Sun-God.** Dikpālas are shown according to their respective directions. 'Pṛthvī' (representation of the terrestrial world) is placed below the higher Bhadrapīṭha, while 'Antarikṣa' (representation of the ethereal world) in the form of lotus is shown above it. Like the Jaina samavasaraṇa, all gods are depicted in **'Vyoman'** and it has been prescribed for worship:

सर्वदेवमयं व्योम कथितं ते महाभुज।
तस्य संपूजनं कृत्वा सर्वान्कामानवाप्नुयात्॥

Most important in the present context, however, is the *VDP* text on **Aiḍūka** (Vol. I, Chapter-84, pp. 220-21; Vol. II, pp. 168-75) which too has been prescribed as an **Architecture** symbolising the Cosmic divinity. It is caturāsra (square) and terraced. The first terrace (Bhadrapīṭha) has stairways (flight of steps) on each side (attached to, or given into it) (i. e. in all the four directions like a Ziggurat). Above it, are two other terraces (bhadrapīṭhas). On the third is built a square structure supported on four pillars or piers having Liṅga form, with thirteen floors (bhūmikas), topped by a spherical form (like dome) which is crowned by āmalasāraka. Sun and Moon must be represented on two sides. The four lokapālas: Virūḍha, Dhṛtarāṣṭra, Virūpākṣa and Kubera, dressed like the Sun and wearing armours and ornaments, must be depicted in the four directions of the floors. These are to be known as Śakra, Yama, Varuṇa and Kubera. Thus are represented the fourteen (mythological) worlds (bhuvanas). The Liṅga form represents Maheśwara (Śiva) the spherical form represents Pitāmaha (Brahmān) and the square form represents Janārdana (Viṣṇu). The Three Bhadrapīṭhas represent three basic elements (guṇas) of the creation: Sattva, Rajas and Tamas. These three bhadrapīṭhas thus indicate the aggregate of the three worlds with their animate and inanimate objects.

This form of Aiḍūka is called 'Prajāhita' or auspicious to the people, i. e. for the welfare of the people, and its worship is recommended for happiness in this world and mokṣa after death:

ऐडूकरूपं   कथितं   मयैतत्,

प्रजाहिताख्यं   यदुवंशमुख्य।

ऐडूकपूजानिरता   लभन्ते

सुखं मनुष्या दिवि वासमन्ते॥

It is the architectural representation of the whole **Cosmic Universe** and its worship is equal to the worship of the whole world, i. e. all divinities. Hence its sanctity.

As Priyabala Shah discussed (Vol. II, pp. 168-75), Aiḍūka was originally associated with cremation and was a pre-Buddhist quadrilateral structure like Ċatuḥ-srakti śmaśāna of the daivī prajā mentioned in the *Śatapatha-Brāhmaṇa*. Like stūpa it also contained bones or ashes. Gradually, from a purely **funereal** structure, it became a **commemorative** structure, in other words, a memorial which in due course of time, with the process of deification, became **votive.**

5. *MĀNA-STAMBHA-PŪJA:* Manuscript No. 7758 (author unknown) cf. *Catalogue* of Sanskrit & Prakrit Mss. in the Central Provinces and Berar, by Hiralal, Nagpur Govt. Press 1926: on the worship of the **Mānastambha** erected by gods at the entrance of the maṇḍapa of the Jaina temple (i. e. like a kīrttistambha).

6. *STŪPA-LAKSANA-KĀRIKĀ-VIVAIÇANAM* by
Bhadravyūha, Ms. cf. *A Catalogue* of Palm-Leaf and Selected
Paper Mss. belonging to Durbar Library Nepal by MM. H. P. Sastri
(Intro. C. Bendall) Vol. II (Calcutta 1915); also cf. Notes of Mss.
from (Bir Library) Nepal, taken by K. M. Varman of Kala-Bhawan
Visva-Bharati 1949 (for full details see Haridas Mitra, *Contribution
to a Bibliography of Indian Art and Aesthetics* (Visva-Bharati,
1980) pp.231-32.

7. APARĀJITAPṚCCHĀ TEXTS ON KĪRTTISTAMBHAS
A. Sutra-LXX (Bhūdharādibrahmanagaram)

सूत्र – ७० भूधरादिब्रहमनगरं

विस्वाद्विपेषुरा   सर्वमाज्ञातं   सांशुभः   निद्रौ ? ।
प्रोक्तस्तम्भो ध्वजास्तम्भः कीर्तिस्तंभो महान्तथा ॥ २५ ॥
षड्विधं   तदधः   पीठं   मालिकास्त्वेकविंशतिः ।
तन्मध्ये   देवताः   सर्वे   स्वर्गपातालवासिनः ॥ २६ ॥
मेरुच्छन्दभवः   स्तम्भो   ब्रह्माण्डसदृशः   पुरः ।
तदुपरि   शिवमूर्तिः   शक्तिस्त्रिज्योतिरूपिणी ॥ २७ ॥
मेरुच्छन्दः   समाख्यातः   विभागान्   शृणु साम्प्रतम् ।
चतुरश्रं   समं   कृत्वा   तारकं   पीठमुत्तमम् ॥ २८ ॥
उक्ताश्च   चतुरशीतिः   कीर्तिस्तम्भा   विभागशः ।
समस्ता   उत्सेधभागाः   शतमष्टोत्तरं   स्मृताः ॥ २९ ॥
तेनभागप्रमाणेन   विस्तारः   स्याच्चतुर्दश ।
तत्वभागैश्च   भद्रार्धं   कर्णश्चैव   द्विभागकः ॥ ३० ॥
पूर्वभद्रे   भवेद्   ब्रह्मा   दक्षिणे   तु   जनार्दनः ।
अनन्तः   पश्चिमे   भद्रे   रुद्रश्चोत्तरतो   दिशि ॥ ३१ ॥
कोणे   भद्रे   तथा   स्तम्भे   सप्तभागसमुच्छ्रिते ।
महाश्रृङ्गाणि   चाष्टैव   मेघाकाराणि   तानि   च ॥ ३२ ॥
सार्धं   भागं   तु   परिधौ   त्यजेच्छृङ्गक्रमेण   वै ।
तदूर्ध्वे   दशभागा   च   इल्लकातौरणैर्युता ॥ ३३ ॥

कोणे   भद्रे   तथा   श्रृङ्गे   यक्षगन्धर्वपन्नगा: ।
भवन्ति ते स्वेच्छया च देवा वा दैत्यदानवा: ॥ ३४ ॥
परिधौ   मत्स्यादिदेवाश्च   तथैकादशरुद्रका: ।
शिवशक्तयोऽनेकाश्च   रूपभेदेन   संस्थिता: ॥ ३५ ॥
सागरा:   पर्वता   द्वीपा   समस्ता   भोगरूपका ।
समुद्रशैलवसना   पृथ्वी   च   सप्तमातर: ॥ ३६ ॥
भूपालश्च   तथा   कल्पवृक्षाश्च   मुनिसत्तमा: ।
वायुश्च   सूर्यचन्द्राद्या: सनक्षत्रा: सराशय: ॥ ३७ ॥
इन्द्रो   रुद्रस्तथोपेन्द्रो   ब्रह्मा   विष्णुस्तथैव   च ।
शैलेयी⋯⋯⋯⋯   शंकरश्च   सदाशिव: ॥ ३८ ॥

B. Sutra - CXLV (Samastadhvajānirṇaya)

सूत्र — १४५. समस्तध्वजानिर्णय

राजप्रवेशे   कर्तव्यं   प्रतोल्यग्रे   सुशोभनम् ।
ध्वजा: स्तम्भगता: कीर्तिपताकाश्चैव हस्तिषु ॥ १० ॥
जयन्तश्च   प्रतापाख्य: कीर्त्यानन्दो   महोत्सव: ।
एकच्छत्रस्तथा कार्या: कीर्तिस्तम्भाश्च पञ्चहि ॥ ११ ॥
एकविंशतिहस्तैश्च   जयन्तो   नाम   नामत: ।
उच्छ्रितश्च   प्रतापस्त्रिचत्वारिंशत्करैस्तथा ॥ १२ ॥
पञ्चषष्ठिकरैश्चैव   स   भवेत्कीर्तिनन्दन: ।
सप्ताशीतिकरैश्चैव   कामदस्तु   महोत्सव: ॥ १३ ॥
नवोत्तरशतहस्तैरेकच्छत्रो   भवेत्तथा ।
एवं   पञ्च   महास्तम्भा   महाराजपुरे   मता: ॥ १४ ॥
पृथुत्वं   चतुर्थांशेन   तत्षडंशेन   चोर्ध्वत: ।
पञ्चमांशेनाध: कुर्यात्   षडंशोच्छ्रयमानत: ॥ १५ ॥
तत्षडंशेन   ऊर्ध्वेषु   ऊर्ध्वमानं   त्रिभूमिकम् ।
वृत्ताकारं   प्रकर्तव्यं   घण्टाकलशसंयुतम् ॥ १६ ॥
दक्षिणे   तत्र   वै   कीर्ति – पताका   हस्तकास्तथा ।
आद्ये   धर्मो   द्वितीये   तु   यश: कीर्तिस्तदूर्ध्वत: ॥ १७ ॥
धर्मयश:कीर्तिदं   स्यादेवं   माडं   त्रिभूमिकम् ।
पीठबन्धोपरि   कुर्यादूर्ध्वे   चैवं   तु   मेखला ॥ १८ ॥

दिक्पाललोकपालानां   वसूनां   च   महत्तमा: ।
चतु:षष्टिश्च दिव्यानां स्वर्गिणां त्वेकविंशति: ॥ १९ ॥
माडोपरि   ध्वजादण्डपताका:   शत्रुमर्दन: ।
एवंविधं प्रकर्तव्यं कीर्तिस्तम्भस्य लक्षणम् ॥ २० ॥
इति कीर्तिस्तम्भलक्षणम् ।

A. Translation   (*AP. LXX. 25-38*)

This aphorism (standard text) belongs to the (North Indian) School (of Architecture) of Visvakarman. He has thus laid down the rules for the construction of the auspicious stambha: Dhvajastambha and Kīrttistambha, as follows (25).

Its pīṭha may be built of six types and Mālikā of twentyone types, all the gods resident of Svarga and Pātāla should be shown between the pīṭha and the Mālikā (26).

This stambha (Dhvajastambha and Kīrttistambha) has originated from the Merucchanda. In form it is like Brāhmāṇḍa. Place an image of Śiva above it representing the three jyotis of Śakti (27).

Now hear, I explain the Merucchanda. It is square (each side being equal in size) and has a Tāraka pīṭha which is the best of all (28).

With such divisions, 84 types of Kīttistambhas can be built. It has 108 parts on the whole vertical axis (29).

According to the proportions of these divisions, it spreads 14 parts on the horizontal axis. Each Bhadra measures half of the main part, while Karṇa is twice of it (30).

Brahmā should be shown on the eastern Bhadra; Janārdana Viṣṇu on the southern, Ananta Viṣṇu on the western and Rudra Śiva on the northern Bhadra respectively (31).

Bhadras, Koṇas (karṇikās) and the Stambha (main shaft) rise seven parts (above the pīṭha). They are crowned above, by eight Meghākāra śṛṅgas (spires) (32).

In the order of these śṛṅgas, around the circumference, one and half parts are left over. Over it, in ten parts, is built the Illikā-Toraṇa (इल्लिका-तोरण) (one on each of the four sides) (33).

Yakṣas, gandharvas, sarpas (and other celestial beings), gods and demons, as desired, may be depicted on Bhadras, Karṇikās and Śṛṅgas (34).

Matsya and other incarnations of Viṣṇu should be shown on the circumference (of the inner main shaft). Similarly 11 Rudras (of Śiva) should be shown. Different forms (viz. icons) of Śiva and Śakti should be appropriately stationed (35).

The Earth along with mountains and oceans which are treasures of all the worldly things and Seven Mothers (Sapta-mātṛikās) should be thus represented on the Kīrttistambha (36).

King, kalpavṛkṣa, ascetics, Vāyu, Sun, Moon, Nakṣatras, Rāśis and gods etc., i. e. all the celestrial phenomena should also be represented suitably on the Kīrttistambha (37).

Indra, Rudra, Upendra, Brahmā, Viṣṇu, Pārvatī, Śiva, Sadāśiva etc. all divine forms should also be duly shown on the Kīrttistambha (38).

B. Translation (*AP. CXLX. 10-20*)

Patākās (flags) should be installed on beautiful dhvajasthambhas in front of the pratolīs (main gateways) through which the King passes, and elephants should also carry them. They denote Kīrtti (10).

Kīrttistambhas are of five types, viz. Jayanta, Pratāpa, Kīrtyanandana, Mahotsava and Ekacchatra (11).

Jayanta is 21 hands in height, Pratāpa is 43 (12).

Kīrttinandana is of 65 hands height, while Mahotsava measures 87 hands (13).

Ekacchatra is the highest Kīrttistambha and it measures 109 hands in height. These five types of regal Kīrttistambhas can be built in the capital (of a sovereign ruler) (14).

Its thickness should be of four parts (of the mean height in each case) and six parts should be built above. Five parts should be below the ground i. e. in foundations and six parts in height (?) (15).

Above the six parts, three storeys should again be built. All this should be crowned by a spherical śikhara with bell and kalaśa (16).

Kīrttipatākā should be installed on its southern side. The three storeys will respectively represent Dharma, Yaśa and Kīrtti (17).

The Māda representing Dharma, Yaśa and Kīrtti should thus be made of three storeys. There should be a Mekhalā over the pīṭhabandha (18).

Thereupon, Dikpālas, Lokapālas, Vasus, 64 gods and 21 svargas (heavens) etc should be depicted (19).

Dhvajā should be installed on the Māḍa for the destruction of enemies. Kīrttistambha should be built in accordance with these characteristics (20).

8. VĀSTU-VIDYĀ TEXT ON KĪRTTISTAMBHAS[1]

श्री विश्वकर्मा उवाच।

नमामि   शारदादेवी   देवमानववंदिताम्।
नामानि   चर्चिता   वक्षे   कीर्तिस्तंभादिलक्षणं॥ 1॥
अनेक   शिल्पी   कार्याणि   सिद्धिकेतु   सुखाप्तये।
कीर्तिस्तंभोमहानाभो   प्रोच्यते   विश्वकर्मणे॥ 2॥
शुद्धभूमितले   स्तंभः   कीर्ति   कर्तव्य   ज्ञायते।
भूमितोऽंकुरपात्राद्यै   श्रेष्टितिश्चामलैरिमै॥ 3॥
नैनारीरूपैश्च   रूपिणी   शतसंयुते।
दिव्यपाषाणसंपत्रे   रंशेर्नानाविधैर्युंते॥ 4॥
प्रभाभूषितशक्तिनां   मध्यकोणता   मुख्यकं।
भद्रकर्णेविकर्णाद्य   वक्षे   वास्तुविचारिनः॥ 5॥
प्रासादेऽग्रेउगणवारे   स्थापित   विश्वकर्मणा।
प्रतोल्यासहितो   देवै   पूजिते   खिलसिद्धिदं॥ 6॥
यस्य   दर्शनमात्रेण   जिनशासनदीपकै।
जिनवर्गोमहापुण्यं   प्राप्यते   भवसागरे॥ 7॥
महाप्रासादकरणे   निष्पन्नै   वास्तुवेदिके।
पूर्णयाये   ततःकार्यो   मानस्तंभसकीर्तिदं॥ 8॥
अभिरूपभरूपश्च   विरूप   मध्यरूपकैः।
कीर्तिस्तंभो   विभातिह   भूमौपुण्यकृतांनृणां॥ 9॥
पूर्वदक्षिण   वारुण्योदिशोवाक्ष   कुबेरका।
चतुरस्रं   कोणकाश्चैव   ईशानाग्निनैरुत्यनिलः॥ 10॥

1.   *Vāstu-Vidyāyāṃ* of Vīśwakarmān (ed. with Gujarati tr. by P. O. Sompura, Ahmedabad, n. d.) pp. 223-26.

ध्रुवसाधन   कामादौ   कीर्तिस्तंभाकारयेत् ।
सर्वे वास्तुकृत: श्रेष्ठं कीर्तिस्तंभस्यलक्षणं ॥ 11 ॥
मानप्रमाण   संयुक्तं   लघुदीर्घसमन्वितं ।
अनुरूप यथायोग्य कर्तव्यं विश्वकर्मणा ॥ 12 ॥
अष्टभाग   विभक्तेन   भूपीठे   सुंदराश्रये ।
भद्रकर्णेविकर्णाटै:   कीर्तिस्तंभोविरच्यते ॥ 13 ॥
सप्तभूमिमयकार्या   वास्तुवेदेत्रिशत्यभी ।
प्रथमभूमिरुदिष्टा   भद्रत्रय   विराजिता ॥ 14 ॥
जाइयकुंभकणालिच   तत्रग्रासपद्यापुन: ।
गजस्थानं नर:स्थानं पुर:स्थानं च कुंभकं ॥ 15 ॥
कलशोऽन्तरपत्रं   च   कपोतमंचिकस्तथा ।
बहिर्जंघाविभागश्च   दिक्पालाश्चसपन्नगा ॥ 16 ॥
अन्तर्जंघा   विभागेन   गणगंधर्वशक्त्यया ।
उद्गाभरणीचैव   कणालिचशिरावटि ॥ 17 ॥
पट्टिकाद्याद्यकूटं   च   मंडोवरादिभूमिका ।
एतस्यो   भूमिकायं   च   उपर्योपरिसूरिभि: ॥ 18 ॥
-- - --- - - - - कर्तव्यंवास्तुविधिनां ।
बाह्यभूमि विभूमिषु पुरुषमूर्ति प्रतिष्ठितं ॥ 19 ॥
एवं   षट्भूमिकायं   च   उपर्यापरिसूरिभि: ।
कर्तव्य वास्तुविधिनां बाह्यभूमिविभूमिषु ॥ 20 ॥
आद्यभूमिमहानन्दा   द्वितीया   नंदबद्धनी ।
तृतीया धर्मविस्तारा चतुर्थ कर्मसिद्धिदा ॥ 21 ॥
पञ्चमी   देवतातुल्या   षष्टिमोक्षस्वरूपका ।
सप्ताभ्यानन्दविवर्णा   अष्टमितुअयोनिजा ॥ 22 ॥
नवभि एकदशीस्यात् एवं च (नव) भूमिलक्षणं ।
शिवालये   शिवकुर्यात्   ब्रह्णंब्रह्णंस्थले ॥ 23 ॥
विष्णुस्थाने   महाविष्णु   जिनेजैनप्रकर्तिना ।
नगरे राजधानी च महादुर्गे विशेषत: ॥ 24 ॥
भूपालयवलभ:स्तंभ: वास्तुशास्त्रे   प्रकर्तिता ।
स्तंभकीर्तिदर्शनेय   तीर्थकोटि   कलफलप्रदं ॥ 25 ॥

Translation

So said Viśwakarmān : Adoration to the Goddess Śārdā (Saraswatī) who is worshipped by gods and men alike. Now I will speak on the architecture of the Kīrttistambhas which are built by expert Śilpīns for happiness. It is founded in perfect ground, free from any defects. Human beings are depicted in it in hundreds of beautiful forms. Perfect stones are procured for its construction and for the making of sculptures. It is adequately planned on the horizontal and the vertical axis with bhadras, karṇas and vikarṇas according to the Vāstu texts. Kīrttistambha must be built along with pratolī in front of the Prāsāda (Temple) for the worship of gods, for success. Kīrttistambha is sacred. It is propitious even to look at it. It bestows puṇya to the devotee and emancipates from the worldly bondage. Hence, it must be built invariably with mahāprāsādas and ornamented with celestial and terrestrial forms. Image of Varuṇa must be installed on its south-east and Kubera on north-west. Agni and other Vedic gods are accordingly placed on other sides and angles of its square plan. Kīrttistambha's is the highest architecture and it must be built strongly and stably, with perfect proportions, laid down by Viśwakarmān. The pīṭha should be divided into eight mouldings, with respective bhadras, and karṇikās. It has seven bhūmis (floors). The First one, i. e. on the pīṭha, has three bhadras, with such traditional vertical mouldings as jāḍyakumbha, grāsapaṭṭī, padma vallarī, gajathara, narathara and kumbhaka, kalaśa, antarpatṛa and kapotālī (exactly like the pīṭha of the Hindu temple). Dikpālas and other figures should be shown on it exteriorly. Jaṁghā should also be divided into traditional mouldings with respective sculptures of gandharvas and other divinities. Paṭṭikā, chādya, kūṭa etc. must be made on the maṇḍovara and appropriate sculptures be shown on it exteriorly. The first bhūmi (floor) is called 'Mahānandā, second 'Nandabaddhanī', third 'Dharmavistāra, fourth 'Karmasiddhadā', fifth 'Devatātulya', sixth 'Mokṣaswarūpakā', seventh 'Abhyānandavivarṇā', eighth 'Ituayonijā' (?), and nineth 'Ekādaśī'. Thus it is built (at the most) in nine storeys. A form of Śiva must preside the kīrttistambha which faces the Śiva temple, of Brahmān which faces Brahmān temple, of Viṣṇu which faces Viṣṇu temple and of Jina which faces Jaina Temple respectively. It must be built invariably in the capital city or capital fort. Kings build kīrttistambhas in accordance with the Vāstu texts for fame (kīrtti). It bestows religious merit equivalent to a karor of tīrthas.

9. DĪPĀRṆAVA[1] TEXT ON KĪRTTISTAMBHAS

अथात: संप्रवक्ष्यामि   कीर्तिस्तंभस्य   लक्षण।

जयन्तश्च प्रतापख्य कीर्तिनन्दो महोत्सव: ॥ 11 ॥
एकच्छत्रस्तथा   कार्या   कीर्तिस्तंभाश्चपंचहि।
एकविंशति यदा हस्तौ जयन्तो नाम नामत: ॥ 12 ॥
प्रतापख्यस्तत्रं   कुर्यात्   त्रयचत्वारि   हस्तकं।
पंचषष्टि   यदाहस्तं   सएव   कीर्तिनंदनं ॥ 13 ॥
सप्ताशिति   हस्तान्तं   तु   महोत्सवै   कीर्तित:।
नवोत्तरशतं   हस्तै   एकछत्रोद्भवास्तथा ॥ 14 ॥
एवं   पञ्चमहास्तंभा   महाराज्ञाद्वा   (?)   पुरे।
पृथुत्वे चतुर्थांशेन तत्षडांशे न चोर्ध्वत् ॥ 15 ॥
पंचमांशे   नाऽध: कुर्यात्   षडांशोच्छ्रय   मानत:।
ऊर्ध्वेषु   माऽमध्र्वतु   त्रिंचतुष्टयं   भूमिकं ॥ 16 ॥

---

1. *Dīpārṇava* of Viśwakarmān (Uttarārdha), ed. and tr. in Gujarati by. P. O. Sompura (Ahmedabad, 1976) pp. 74-77.

तत् षडांशेन ऊर्ध्वेषु ऊर्द्धमानं त्रिभूमिकम्।
वृत्ताकारं प्रकर्तव्यं घंटा कलशं संयुतम्।
दक्षिणे कीर्तिपताका वामे कीर्तिस्तदध्वंत्॥ 17 ॥
एवं त्रिभूमोद्भव मांड धर्मकीर्ति यशोद्भं।
पीठबंधस्तत: कुर्यात्ध्वेतस्यैव मेखला:॥ 18 ॥
दिक्पाल: लोकपालश्च बसंतानां च महोत्सव:।
चतु:षष्टिश्वदेवानां स्वगुणात्वेकविंशति॥ 19 ॥
मांडोपरि ध्वजा कार्या दण्डपताकामर्कटि।
एवं विधेयं कर्तव्यं इति कीतिस्तंभलक्षणम्॥ 20 ॥
तडाजं च महायज्ञे ध्वत्रास्तंभ समोद्भवा।
आनंदो दुन्दुभि: कान्तंश्रीमुखसुमनोहरं॥ 21 ॥
नवहस्तो भवेदाद्य सप्तदशकरोन्नत।
तदग्रे कलश कुर्याद्ध्वजावंश समन्वितं॥ 22 ॥
वापिषु दक्षिणेद्वारे ध्वजस्तंभ प्ररोपयेत्।
पीठबंध सुकर्तव्या एकद्द्वित्रिकरोन्नत॥ 23 ॥
त्रिहस्त पंचसप्त समुन्नत तदूर्ध्वेकलशं दिव्य।
कुंडेषु पुष्करे कूपे ध्वजस्तंभसमुद्भवेत्॥ 24 ॥
त्रिपञ्व सप्तहस्तांन्ते उदकांन्रर शतशुभं।
तथा प्राचि मिशान मध्ये विभजे नवभागत:।
वामे त्रयं परित्यजे दक्षिणे च त्रयत्यनेत्॥ 25 ॥

Translation

Now I will speak on the architecture of the kīrttistambhas which are of five types : (1) *Jayanta* of 21 hands, (2) *Pratāpa* of 43 hands, (3) *Kīrttinandana* of 65 hands, (4) *Mahotsava* of 87 hands and (5) *Ekachatra* of 109 hands in elevation (Udaya). These five types of kīrttistambhas are built in the capital city of the king. These are built in proportion to these measurements of the elevation. The base is its fourth part while superstructure is its sixth part in thickness (length and breadth which are equal, as it is a square) thus decreasing in size as it rises. Upper part may be made in three, four or eight bhūmis (floors) (?). A mānda, miniature mandapa or chhatrī, of three floors should be given in the sixth part of the elevation. It should be surmounted by a spherical roof crowned by ghantā and kalaśa. Patākā should be placed on its right side and kīrttistambha on the left (?). The kīrttistambha of three-floor mānda is propitious for dharma, yaśa and kīrtti. Suitable mouldings must be carved on the pīthabandha. Dikpālas, lokapālas, 64 gods and 21 divine forms must be depicted on them. Dhvaja, danda, patākā and markati must be placed on the mānda. Thus the kīrttistambhas should be made.

10. The **(1)** *PRABANDHA-CARITRA,* **(2)** *PRABANDHA CINTĀMANI* **AND** *PURĀTANA-PRABANDHA-SANGRAHA;* **(3)** *PRABANDHA- KOSA;* **and (4) VIVIDHA-TĪRTHA-KALPA** are some of the basic texts on geographical and historical Jaina tīrthas, including such subjects as 'Nandīśvara-Dwīpa', 'Samavasarana' and 'Astāpada'. Thus the *Vividha-Tīrtha-Kalpa* which was composed by Jinaprabha Sūri in the 14th century A.D. (Part-I,

ed. by Muni Jinavijaya, Shanti Niketan 1934) describes the
'Aṣṭāpada-Mahātīrtha- Kalpa' (Chapter-18, p. 31 in Sanskrit);
'Nandīśvara-Dwīpa- Kalpa' (Chapter-24, pp.48-49 in Sanskrit);
'Samavasaraṇa-Raçanā-Kalpa' (Chapter-46, pp. 87-88 in
Prakrit); and 'Aṣṭāpada - Giri - Kalpa' (Chapter-49, pp. 91-93
in Prakrit) in complete details as structures symbolising 'Jagat'.
An Analytical study of these references in these and other works
published under the Singhi-Jaina-Grantha-Mala has yet to begin
in the right earnest. The construction and worship of these
symbolic structures has been alluded to in these historical
'prabandhas' over and over again. For example, Samavasaraṇas
are referred to in the year V.S. 1335 / 1278 A.D. at Chittorgadh
during   the   reign   `of   Samarasiṁha   in   the
Kharatara-Gaçcha-Brhad-Gurvāvali (ed. Muni Jinavijaya Bombay
1956, p. 56), almost contemporaneous to the *JKS*.

APPENDICES

(C). TABLES ON ANCIENT PILLARS AND STRUCTURES

1. Table on Ancient Pillars
2. Table on Ancient Structures

1. Ancient Pillars

		I Functional/ Symbolic	II Monolithic/ Structural	III Sectarian Affiliation
1.	*Stambha*	Functional central Pillar of the house of the Vedic period	Wooden monolithic	Secular
2.	*Yūpa-Stambha*	Vedic ritualistic Pillar associated with the yajnas	Wooden monolithic	Vedic Dharma
3.	*Skambha*	Symbolic Vedic pillar denoting the cosmic order	Vedic monolithic (Conceptual)	Vedic thought and philosophy
4.	*Dhvaja-Stambha*	Symbolic Hindu and Buddhist Pillar	Hindu Stone monolithic	Hindu & Buddhist
5.	*Dharma-Stambha (Lat)*	Buddhist sacred Pillar, religious and symbolic	Stone monolithic	Buddhist

6.	*Kīrtti-Stambha*	Symbolic Hindu Pillar bearing Vāhana of Śaiva or Vaiṣṇava worship, later associated with the Sūrya-Puruṣa concept of the world sustenance: "Alambaṃ-stambhaṃ- ekaṃ Tribhuwana-Bhuwanasya"	Stone monolithic	Hindu (Śaiva & Vaiṣṇava); it is classical
7.	*Māna-Stambha* Or *Mānasa-Stambha* Or Mānavaka-Stambha	Symbolic Jaina Pillar bearing an image of the Tīrthankara or his Vāhana	Stone monolithic	Jaina
8.	*Goverdhana-Stambha*	Memorial Pillars of the deified heroes bearing images of such gods as Sūrya, Gaṇeśa, Kṛṣṇa and Śiva, of a sacred character	Stone monolithic	Essentially Hindu; it is folk rather than classical

NOTE 1. These are all **monolithic** pillars, in the *Sūcikāçhanda,* which rose **vertically.** Each one was Technically a **Sculpture.**

2. Ancient Structures

	I. Plan	II. Elevation	III. Purpose	IV. Form	V. References
1.	**Ziggurat (Jārūka) Ancient West Asiatic (Assyrian) Structure**	Çaturāsra (square)	Multi-Terraced with stairways	Probably originally *funereal,* later *votive*	It was an Architecture	See 'Bibliography & Notes'
2.	**Aiḍūka Ancient Indian (probably inspired by Ziggurat) Funereal Structure**	Çaturāsra	Multi-Terraced (Bhadrapīṭhas)	Originally funereal, later became *votive*	It was an Architecture	See *VDP* text (vide *Appendix* : (B) 4
3.	**Stūpa Ancient Indian (Jaina, Buddhist & Hindu) Funereal Structure**	Initially both Çaturāsra and Vrttākāra (circular) plans were used, later only circular plan came into vogue	Even in the spherical form, it is associated with gateways in the four directions, stairways, galleries and a composite superstructure	Originally funereal, later became commemorative and votive	It was an Architecture	See 'Bibliography & Notes'

4.	Samavasaraṇa (Ancient Jaina)	Çaturāsra	Multi-terraced (Bhadrapīṭhas)	Associated with the nirvāna of the Jinas, hence originally Funereal and commemorative later became votive	It was an Architecture	See texts referred to in Appendix (B)
5.	Aṣṭāpada (Jaina)	Çaturāsra	Eight storeyed (Bhadrapīṭhas)	Symbolised the Jaina mythological concept of Jagat (Universe) in a limited sense, which was used for worship (votive)	It was an Architecture	See texts referred to in Appendix (B)
6.	Meru-Giri & Nandīśvara - Dwīpa (Jaina)	Vṛttākāra (Circular)	Multi-terraced (Bhadrapīṭhas)	Symbolised the Jaina philosophical concept of Jagat (Universe) like the Brahmanical 'Meru' in a subtle sense, it was also votive	It was an Architecture	See texts referred to in Appendix (B)

| 7. | Meru ' _umeru) (Brahmanical) | Çaturāsra & Vṛttākāra both | Multi-Terraced (Bhadrapīṭhas) | Symbolical representation of Ṭrailokya or Jagat (Universe) like Viśwarūpa | It was an Architecture | See Vāstu-texts as the *Aparājitaprçcha* which describe it in full details |
| 8. | Vyoman (Brahmanical) | Çaturāsra | Multi-Terraced (Bhadrapithas) | Votive, associateo with Sun-worship | It was an Architecture | See *VDP* text vide *Appendix* (B) 4 |

Note 2. These were all structures in the *Meruçchanda* which spread horizontally. Each one was technically an Architecture.

Note 3.   The structures of Table (C) 2 are not only interconnected but are also
different expressions of the same idea, concept or belief, being a
multi-terraced structure, symbolising the Jagat (Universe) with all
Sūkṣma (subtle) and Sthūla (gross) phenomena of the Sṛṣṭi (Creation)
brought together at one place for human worship. Some of these were
originally (1) **funereal** while others were mythological or philosophical
representations of the World Concept (Trailokya); (2) the funereal
structures gradually became **commemorative**; (3) finally, these
structures became **votive**. Three basic characteristics of these structures
are their: I. Çaturāsra (Sarvatobhadra or Çaumukha) plan; II.
multi-terraced elevation; and III. **Sopāna-Paddhati** (provision of stairs
on the four sides). Note that the Çaturāsra plan is common to Ziggurat,
Aiḍūka, Samavasaraṇa, Aṣṭāpada and Meru (Sumeru) (and the *JKS*).

Note 4.   The two concepts, of Pillar and Structure, first ran parallel and were
shown **together** in the ancient ages as Egyptian Obelisk and Temple;
Assyrian Pillar and Ziggurat; Buddhist Lat and Stūpa; the Tower of Pisa
and Cathedral; the Minaret' al-Malwiya of Samarra and the Mosque;
and the Hindu Dhvajastambha and the Prāsāda, and then coalesced,
integrated and merged in a single thing during the Medieval period,
e.g. in the 13th century A.D. in the *JKS* with the provision of an inner
stairway (which was an architectural innovation) and its emphasis on
the vertical axis, so that the structure was absorbed in the pillar. When
monolithic Kīrttistambha was integrated into its form, it was also
associated with Sun worship as is the structural Kīrttistambha of
Maharana Kumbha at Chittorgadh.

BIBLIOGRAPHY & NOTES

1. **Agarwal, R. C.** : 'Pashchimī Rājasthān-ke kuchh Prārambhik Smriti-Stambha' (Hindi) *Varda* Bissau, VI. 2 (April 1963) 68-79

Deals elaborately with Memorial Pillars of Western Rajasthan

2. **Agarwal, R. C.** : 'Rājasthan-ke Yūpa-Stambha tathā Vedic Yajna' (Hindi) *Nagri Pracharini Patrika* Varanasi, LIX. 2 (V. S. 2011 / 1954 A. D.) 116-22

On the Early Yūpa-pillars of Rajasthan

3. **Agarwal, V. S.** : 'Kīrtti, Kīrttimukha aur Kīrttistambha' (Hindi) *Nagri Pracharini Patrika* Varanasi, LXI-1 (V. S. 2013/1956 A. D.) 64-70; also published in *Bharati* Varanasi No. 1 (1956-57) 92-96

Classical enumeration of symbolism and meaning of the Kīrttistambha Architecture

4. **Ayyar, K. Balasu-** : 'The Memorable Message of the
   brahmanya Heliodorus Column at Besnagar' *Journal of Oriental Research* Madras, XV, Part-III (March 1946) 135-37

Deals with an interesting passage of its inscription

5. **Banerjea, J. N.** : 'Indian Votive and Memorial Columns' *Journal of Indian Society of Oriental Art* Calcutta V (1937) 13-20

6. **Banerjee, N. R.**   : 'Eḍūka   (or   Terraced   and Multiple-roofed Temples)'
                           Bharati Varanasi, Nos. 12-14 (1968-71) 81-110, 5 pls

On Aiḍūka or Ancient Indian Architectural form which was originally funereal and later became votive; extremely useful enumeration

7. **Barua, B. M.**   : 'Stūpa and Tomb'
                           Indian Historical Quarterly, II. 1 (1926) 16-27

8. **Bhandarkar, D. R.**: 'The Kīrttistambha of Rana Kumbha'
                           Journal of Indian Society of Oriental Art Calcutta, I (1933) 52-56

9. **Bhandarkar, D. R.**: 'Jaina Iconography: Samavasaraṇa'
                           Indian Antiquary XL. (1911) 125-30, 153-61

Continued from the Annual Report of the Archaeological Survey of India 1905-6

10. **Boner, Alice**   : 'The Symbolic Aspect of Form'
                           Journal of Indian Society of Oriental Art Calcutta, XVII (1949) 42-50

11. **Chandarwakar,**   : 'Halvad-na Sati-na Paliya ane Daheriyo'
    Pushkar   (Gujarati)
                           Swadhyaya Baroda, VII. 3 (May 1970) 240-47, 5 pls

On the Sati pillars and Chattris at Halvad near Surendranagar in Gujarat

12. **Coedes, George** : 'Note on the Pillar at Sarnath'
                           Journal of Indian Society of Oriental Art Calcutta, V (1937) 40-41

13. **Coomaraswamy,** : *Symbolism of Indian Architecture* (The
    A. K.   Skambha and the Stūpa) (Jaipur 1983)
    Deals with the vertically rising *Skambha* (Pillar) and the
    spherically spreading *Stūpa* and enumerates their symbolism,
    e.g. Architectural Representation of the World Creation or
    'Ekastambha' (Ūnitary Pillar) representation of the World
    Sustenance through the Sun's daily journey

14. **Cousens, Henry** : *A. S. I.* Annual report 1905-6,
                          pp.43-49 :
    a useful article on the restoration of the Jaina Kīrttistambha,
    with excellent illustrations

15. **Dasgupta, P. C.** : 'A Rare Jaina Icon from Sat Deuliya'
                          The Jain Journal Calcutta, VII. 3
                          (January 1973) 130-32
    He studies a unique stele of black basalt depicting the 1st
    Jaina Tīrthankara Rsabhanātha at the crest and rows of other
    tīrthankaras below (in seven terraces) (of 10th century A. D.
    from Burdwan, W. B.). Rsabha is seated while lower panels
    depict Kāyotsarga Tīrthankara. The author quotes U. P. Shah
    on stūpa, samavasarana and ziggurat. Bharata made the first
    stūpa and shrine on the mountain on which Rsabhanātha
    obtained nirvāna. It was an Astāpada of eight terraces. Thus
    grew the concept of an eight-terraced stūpa or ziggurat.
    Dasgupta concludes that this stele is an early representation
    of the Astāpada-Tīrtha in conformity with the Jaina belief and
    symbolism. He also refers to Aidūka.

16. **Dasgupta, P. C.** : 'Stūpa in Mexican Art'
                          The Jain Journal Calcutta, XII. 2
                          (October 1977) 51-60, 5 figures
    Examines the equivalence of its symbolism to Jaina stūpa,
    Çaitya-Yūpa, Jārūka or Aidūka (Ziggurat) in a very
    thought-provoking manner

17. **De, Sudhin**   : 'Çaumukha a Symbolic Jaina Art'
                            The Jaina Journal Calcutta, VI. 1 (July
                            1971) 27-30, 4 pls

He studies the auspicious Sarvatobhadrikā which is visible from all sides. It bears images of four tīrthankaras : 1st Tīrthankara Ṛsabhanātha, 16th Śāntinātha, 23rd Pārśvanātha and 24th Mahāvīra in the four directions. Probably this form is based on ancient Jaina tradition of Samavasaraṇa which was a square (çaturāsra) or circular (terraced) assembly erected by gods for the sermon of the Jina, wherein on a raised platform in the centre sits the Jina on one side with images of the same Jina installed on the three remaining sides to make him visible to the whole audience on all sides. Çaumukha pratimā may thus be a representation of samavasaraṇa. Worship of Çaumukha pratimās was prevalent among the Jainas and various representations are available from all over the country. De cites four examples from West Bengal. (Also see S. K. Saraswati's paper: 'Jaina Motif in Indian and Eastern Architecture' read in the Jaina Seminar at Calcutta, held December 1973, vide its Report in the *Jain Journal* Calcutta, VIII. 3 (January 1974) 129-30. He deals with Sarvatobhadra style and its growth, and a four-faced image called Çaturamukha or Çaumukha which suits well in a sarvatobhadra prāsāda).

18. **Digby, Simon**   : 'The Bhūgola of Ksema-Karaṇa: A dated
                            Sixteenth Century Piece of Indian
                            Metalware'
                            Art & Archaeology Research Papers
                            London, II. 2 (December 1973) 10-31,
                            19 pls

On Indian Cosmology; that it is dated in the 16th century, the age of Akbar, is significant

19. **Dikshitar, V.R.R.** : 'Origin and Early History of the Çaityas'
Indian Historical Quarterly, XIV. 3 (1938) 440-51

20. **Ghosh, A.** : 'Pillars of Aśoka: Their Purpose'
East & West Rome, XVII (1967) 273-75

21. **Govinda, A. B.** : 'Some Aspects of Stūpa Symbolism'
Journal of Indian Society of Oriental Art Calcutta II (1934) 87-105; IV (1936) 25-44

22. **Harshe, R. G.** : 'Mount Meru: The Homeland of the Aryans'
Vishveshvaranand Indological Journal Hoshiarpur II. 1 (March 1964) 135-61

Deals with the concept of Meru: also discusses ancient Town Planning and related architectural subjects

23. **Irwin, John** : 'Asokan Pillars' (I. Reassessment of Evidence; II. Sculpture; and III. Capitals)
The Burlington Magazine London Nos. 115-117 (1973-75) pp. 706-20, 712-27 etc.

Deals with the symbolism of these pillars

24. **Jain, K. P.** : 'Chittor-ka Jaina Kīrttistambha' (Hindi)
Jain Siddhanta Bhaskar Arrah, XIII. 2 (January 1947) 136-37

On the Jaina Kīrttistambha of Chittorgadh built c. 1300 A.D.

25. **Jain, K. P.** : 'Jaina Stūpas at Mathura'
Indian Historical Quarterly, VI. 2 (1930) 376-77

26. **Jastrow, Morris**   : *'The Civilization of Babylonia & Assyria'*
(Philadelphia, 1915)

Also deals elaborately with Ziggurat

27. **Kantawala, S. G.** : 'The Flaming Pillar in Purāṇas'
Vishveshvaranand Indological Journal
Hoshiarpur XII (1972) 152-61

On the Concept of Mount Meru

28. **Khare, M. D.**   : 'Discovery of a Vishnu Temple near the
Heliodoros Pillar, Besnagar (Vidisha)'
Lalit Kala New Delhi, No. 13 (1967)
21-27, 2 pls & 1 fig,

with a conjectural restoration of the superstructure c. 3rd
century B. C.

29. **Kramrisch, Stella :** 'The Four-Cornered Citadel of the Gods
(āyātayali........etaṃ   caturāsraṃ
devapuraṃ B.S.S. 1519)
*Journal of the American Oriental
Society* Baltimore, LXXV. 3 (1955)
184-87

30. **Kramrisch, Stella :** 'Eka-Vrātya, the Conceptual Monument
of Rudra'
*Journal of the Indian Society of Oriental
Art* Calcutta, VIII (1976-77) 9-15

31. **Lishk, S. S. &**   : 'Notion of Obliquity of Ecliptic implied
Sharma, S. D.   in the Concept of Mt. Meru in
Jambūdvīpa Prajnapti'
The Jain Journal Calcutta, XII. 3
(January 1978) 79-92, 4 figs

Examines 'Meru' and its astronomical symbolism with
reference to the Qutb Minar; extremely useful for the study
of the concept of Ziggurat, stūpa, samavasaraṇa and Meru

32. **Lodha, Gopilal**   : 'Vijaya-Stambha : Ek Parichaya' (Hindi)
                           Shodh-Patrika   Udaipur,   XXVII.   3
                           (July-September 1976) 57-60

A brief introduction to the Kīrttistambha of Chittorgadh built
by Maharana Kumbha, erroneously called Vijaya-Stambha
(Victory Tower)

33. **Majumdar, B.**   : 'Symbology of the Aśoka Pillar Capital,
                           Sarnath'
                           Indian Culture Calcutta, II (1935-36)
                           160-63

34. **Maxwell, T.S.**   : 'Transformational Aspects of Hindu
                           Myth and Iconology : "VIŚVARŪPA"
                           Art & Archaeology Research Papers
                           London, II. 2 (December 1973) 59-79,
                           10 pls

Cites examples from texts and sites; also see his article : 'The
Deogarh Viśvarūpa: A Structural Analysis' *AARP*, IV. 2
(December 1975) 8-23, 20 pls; an excellent study of the
symbols and philosophies of architecture

35. **Mitra, A. K.**   : 'The   Mauryan   Lats   or
                           Dhvaja-Stambhas : Do they constitute
                           an Independent Order ?'
                           Journal of the Asiatic Society of Bengal
                           Calcutta   2nd   Series   XXVII   (1933)
                           317-26

36. **Nath, R.**   : *Chittorgadh Kīrttistambha of Maharana
                           Kumbha* (under publication)

Its chapter VI : 'Mahāmeru-Kīrttistambha'; VII : Vedic Skambha
and 'Trailokya-Mahāgrha' and VIII : Garuda and Janārdana
Dhvaja-Stambha deal with the symbolism of the Kīrttistambha
in details

37. **Nath, R.**   : 'The Minaret versus the Dhvajastambha'
                               Indica Bombay, VII. 1 (March 1970)
                               19-31, 5 figs

Traces the origin of the manārah (mīnār or minaret) vis-a-vis
the skambha, dhvaja-stambha and kīrtti-stambha

38. **Pal, Pratapaditya** : 'The Aiḍūka of the Viṣṇu-Dharmottara-
                               Purāṇa and Certain Aspects of Stūpa
                               Symbolism'
                               *Journal of the Indian Society of Oriental
                               Art* Calcutta (New Series) IV
                               (1971-72) (Dr V. S. Agarwal
                               Commemoration Volume Part-I) 49-62

39. **Przyluski, J.**   : 'The Harmikā and the Origin of Buddhist
                               Stūpas'
                               Indian Historical Quarterly, XI.2 (1935)
                               199-210

40. **Satyaprakash**   : 'A Note on the Yūpa Pillars of Rajasthan'
                               *Journal of the Rajasthan Institute of
                               Historical Research* Jaipur, IV.3 (1968)
                               1-7

41. **Settar, S. &**   : *Memorial Stone : A Study of Their Origin,*
    Sontheimar G. D.   *Significance and Variety*
    (editors)   (Dharwad Institute of Indian Art History
                               Dharwad 1982) pp.394, 160 illus

Useful collection of 34 papers on Memorial stones

42. **Shah, Priyabala.**   : 'Aiḍūka'
                               Journal of Oriental Institute Baroda, I.3
                               (1952) 278-85

Deals with various aspects of Aiḍūka, the terraced pyramidal
structure prescribed in the *Viṣṇu-Dharmottara - Purāṇa*

43. **Shah U. P.**   : 'Jaina Bronzes from Cambay'
                          Lalit Kala New Delhi No.13 (1967)
                          31-34, **Figs.15-16** depict bronze
                          Samavasaraṇa (d. 1197 A.D.) from
                          Combay and **Fig.17** bronze
                          Samavasaraṇa (of 1053-60 A.D.) from
                          Sirohi

44. **Shah, U. P.**   : *Studies in Jaina Art*
                          (Banares 1955)

He deals with Jaina tradition of erecting stūpas (pp.9-10, 54, 58, 62-64) mānastambhas (pp.23, 60-61), caityas, caitya-yūpas and stambhas (40-51) Jārūka (Ziggurat) and Samavasaraṇa (56-57, 84-95) and gives a separate Appendix: 'Note on Stūpa, Samavasaraṇa and Ziggurat' (123-129). He noted (p.56) that Yakṣa shrine was an open square hall supported on four pillars, which was prototype of the gandhakuṭī of a Jina in his Samavasaraṇa. This was inspired by Jārūka or Ziggurat (or Aiḍūka). It is not correct to suggest that Aiḍūkas are Brahmanical or Vedic in origin as Priyabala Shah did. U.P. Shah discussed the point elaborately and observed that Samavasaraṇa was based upon the architecture of stūpa which later had the Ziggurat as its prototype with three or more tiers (terraces). The stūpa and the Ziggurat or the Samavasaraṇa were open or visible on all sides. The Gandhakuṭi is the pavilion, open on all the four sides, on a dais in the centre of the Samavasaraṇa. In it was installed the image of the Jina which was visible on all sides (i. e. it was Caumukha). The Jaina Samavasaraṇa was also square or circular in plan and resembled the funereal mound (śmaśāna), referred to in the *Satapatha-Brāhmaṇa*. Shah finally noted: "Samavasaraṇa faithfully preserves the plan of stūpa as also their essentials and it seems the popularity of representations of Samavasaraṇa ultimately replaced the stūpa-symbolism in Jaina worship" (p.57).

45. **Sharma, B.B.** : 'Rawal Chachigdev Pratham-ke ullekhwala.....Shilalekha' (Hindi)
Varda Bissau, XXII.2-3 (April-September 1979) 3-8

Also deals with Goverdhan Memorial pillars (pp.5-6)

46. **Solanki, P.L.** : 'Pallu Ghati aur uski Kalakritiyan' (Hindi)
Varda Bissau, IV.2 (April 1961) 18-26

Deals with Goverdhan Memorial pillars (pp.25-26)

47. **Solomon, E.A.** : 'Skambha-Hymns of the *Atharva-Veda*' (X.7-8)
Journal of Oriental Institute Baroda, IX (1959-60) 233-42

48. **Somani, R.V.** : 'Chittor aur Digambar Jain Sampradaya' (Hindi)
Shodh-Patrika Udaipur, XVI.3-4 (July-October 1965) 96-104

Also deals with the 13th century Jaina Kīrttistambha of Chittorgadh

49. **Sompura, P.O. &** : 'Svargārohaṇa-Prāsāda' (Gujarati)
   Dhaky, M.A.   *Swadhyaya* Baroda, V.2 (February 1968) 191-95

Memorial or commemorative temples as described in the architectural text: *'Śrī-Jñāna-Ratna-Kośa'*; a very useful discovery on the subject

50. **Srivastava, V. S.** : 'Ola (Jaisalmer)-ke Mahatvapurna Goverdhan - Stambha' (Hindi)
Rajasthan Bharati Bikaner, XVIII.3-4 (July. December 1976) 123-130

Useful information on the free-standing symbolic pillars (Goverdhana Memorial Pillars)

51. **Taddei, Maurizio** : 'Inscribed Clay Tablets and Miniature Stūpa from Ghaznin'

East & West Rome, XX (1970) 70-86

Study of the things of the predecessor art, ideas and symbols of which were inherited by the medieval people

52. **Tiwari, M.N.P.** : 'Jaina Samavasaraṇa-ka Pratima Shastriya Adhyayan' (Hindi)

Shodh-Patrika Udaipur, XXIX.3-4 (July-December 1978) 21-24

Samavasaraṇa means assembly made by gods (Deva-Nirmita-Sabhā) where all living beings assemble to hear Jina sermons. Gods make Samavasaraṇa just after the nirvāṇa of jinas (this much of funereal character it possesses). According to Digambar *Mahāpurāṇa*, Indra himself built samavasarana for the Jinas. It is an Architecture, rather than a sculpture. Jina Samavasaraṇa is mentioned from 7th century A.D. onwards. Independent Samavasaraṇas are built in Gujarat and Rajasthan on a large scale.

The form of Samavasaraṇa has been described in the *Ādipurāṇa, Trasaṣṭi - Śalākā - Puruṣa - Caritra* and other Jaina works. He quotes from U. P. Shah to associate it with ziggurat and stūpa. He also quotes from other authorities to describe the Samavasaraṇa (p.22 ftn.3). It is a three-terraced structure with the main Jina sitting on Siṁhāsana facing East. It is associated with eight phenomena : Pratihārya (प्रतिहार्य); Aśoka Vṛkṣa (अशोक-वृक्ष); Sura-Puṣpa - Vṛṣṭi (सुर - पुष्प - वृष्टि); Divya-Dhvani (दिव्य-ध्वनि); Cāmaradhara - Siṁhāsana (चामरधर-सिंहासन); Prabhāmaṇḍala (प्रभामण्डल); Trichatra (त्रिछत्र) and Nagāḍāvādaka (नगाड़ावादक) (being insignia of royalty and divinity). Three other Jina images are installed facing other directions so that the audience could see him from all sides. Every terrace has four entrances protected by armed gate-keepers. On the main terrace, instead of male pratihāras, Goddesses: Jayā, Vijayā, Ajitā and Aparājitā are installed as pratihāras. Flying secondary gods and siddhas are depicted on doors and walls of the first terrace, animals on the second and animals, human and celestial beings on the third. Even lion and deer are shown together without any hostility. The part over the three terraces is built in the form of the śikhara of a temple. Four Jina images in Padmāsana are made upon it. Samavasaraṇa of Mahāvīra temple of Kumbharia (11th century) and Samavasaraṇa of the Devakulikā of Vimala-Vasahi (Abu) (12th century) are important examples.

53. **Walsh, E.H.C.**   : 'Virakal and Sati Memorial Stones at
                           Buddhpur and Buram'
                           *Journal of Bihar & Orissa Research
                           Society* Patna XXIII (1937) 429-443,
                           2 pls

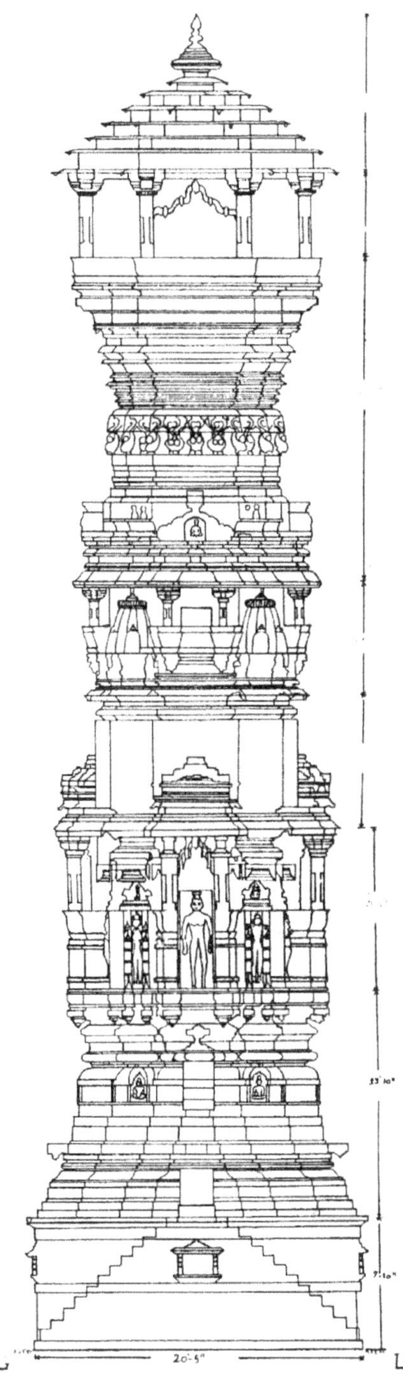

1. Jaina Kīrttistambha (JKS) Chittorgadh : One-side Elevation

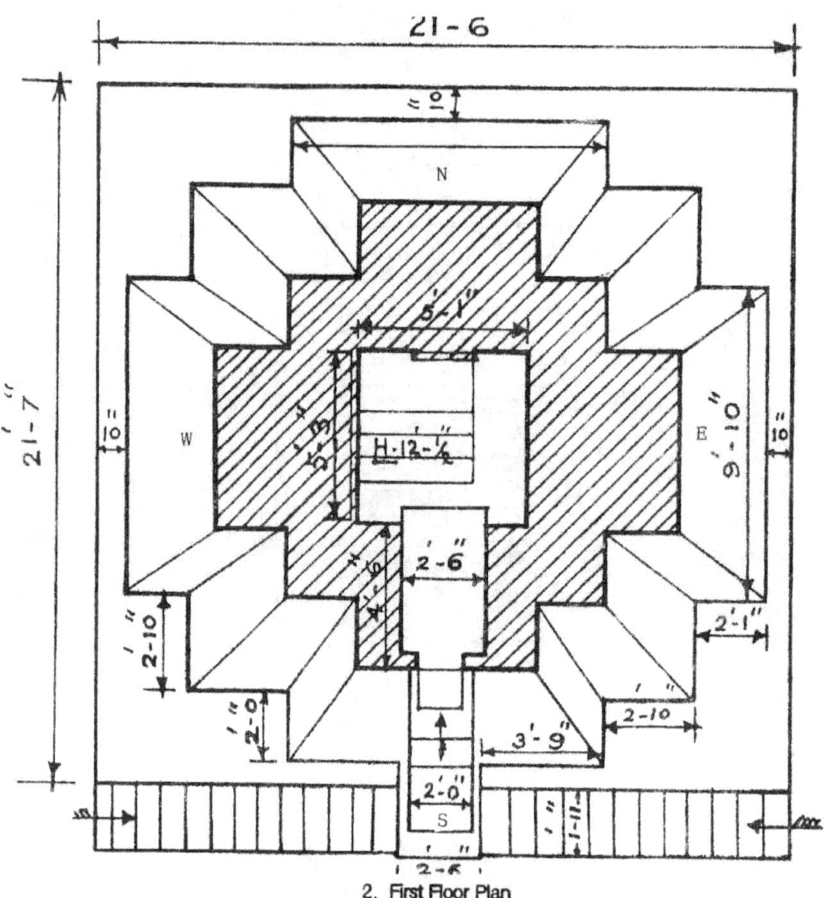

2. First Floor Plan

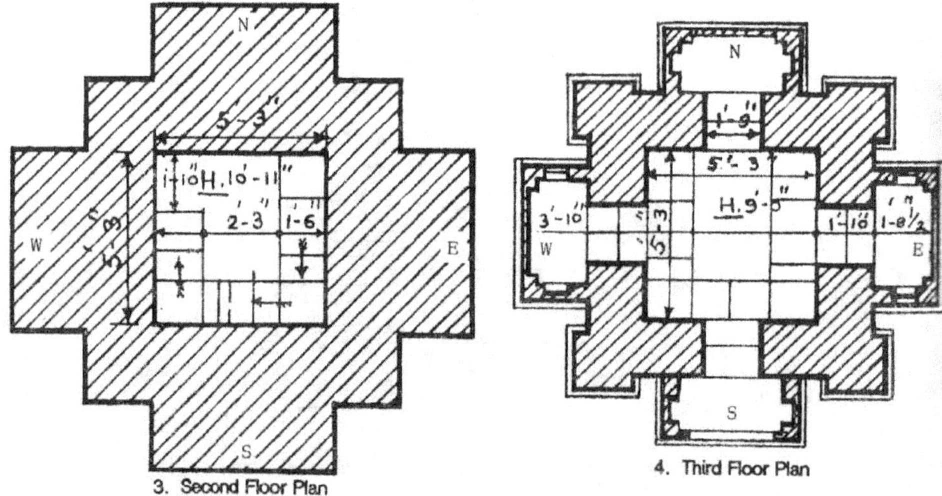

3. Second Floor Plan

4. Third Floor Plan

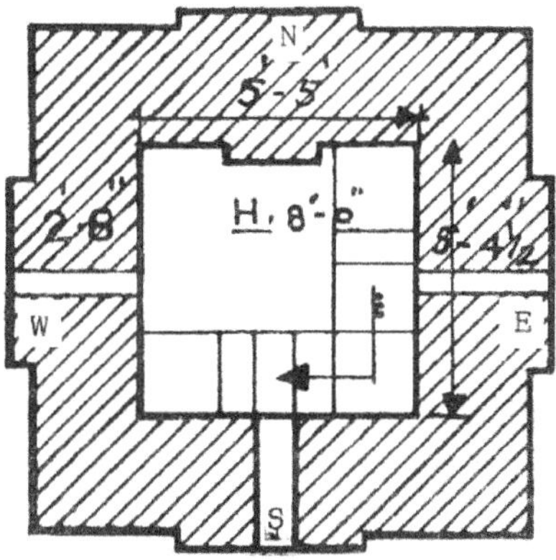

5. Fourth Floor Plan

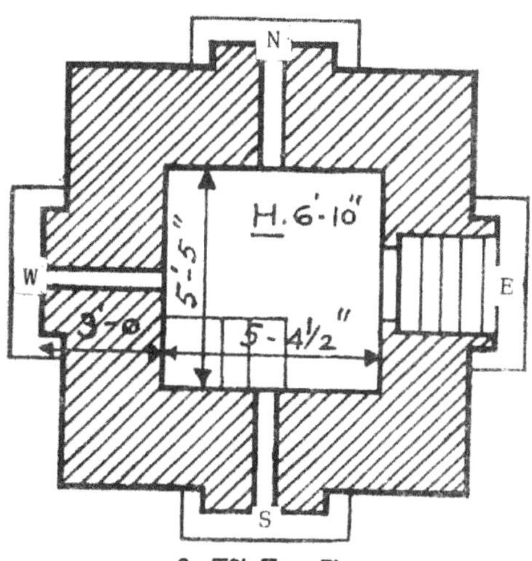

6. Fifth Floor Plan

7. Sixth Floor Plan

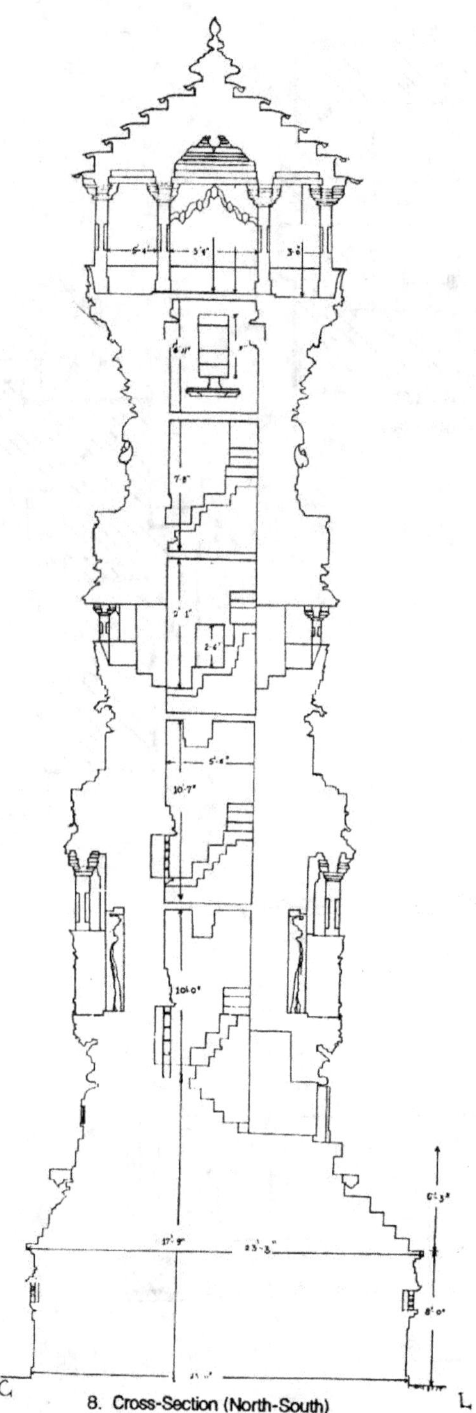

8. Cross-Section (North-South)

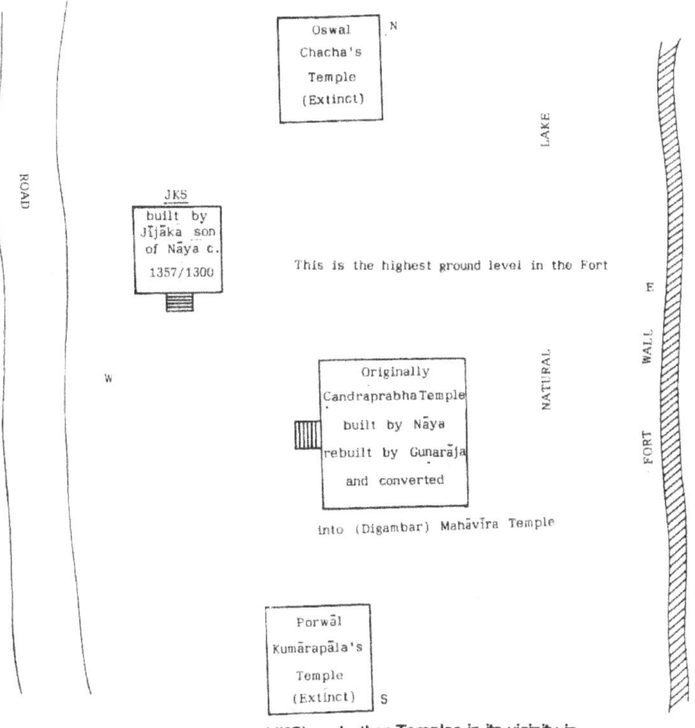

9. Situation of the (**JKS**) and other Temples in its vicinity in V.S. 1485/1428 A.D.

10. 'Parikara' (cf. *Dīpārnava*)

11. 'Samavasaraṇa' (cf. *Dīpārṇava*)

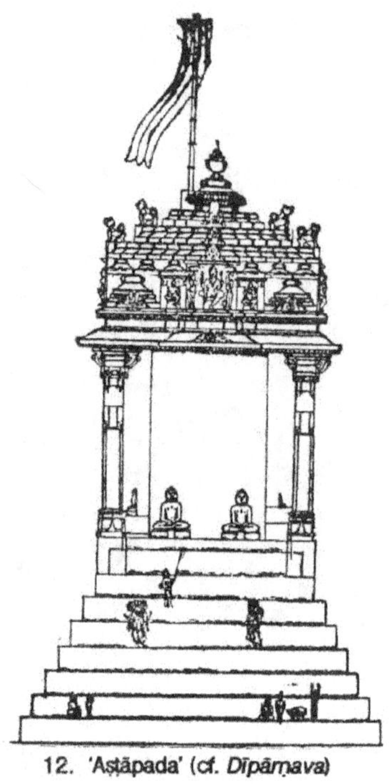

12. 'Aṣṭāpada' (cf. *Dīpārṇava*)

13. Merugiri (cf. Diparnava)

14. 'Nandīśvara-Dwīpa' (cf. *Dīpārṇava*)

15. Bronze Samavasarana (d. 1097 A.D.) from Cambay : Sideview

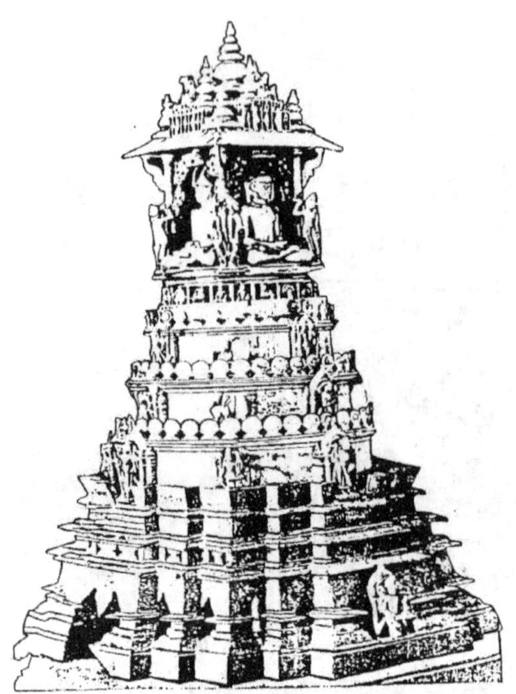

16. Bronze Samavasaraṇa (d. 1097 A.D.) from Cambay :
    Corner View

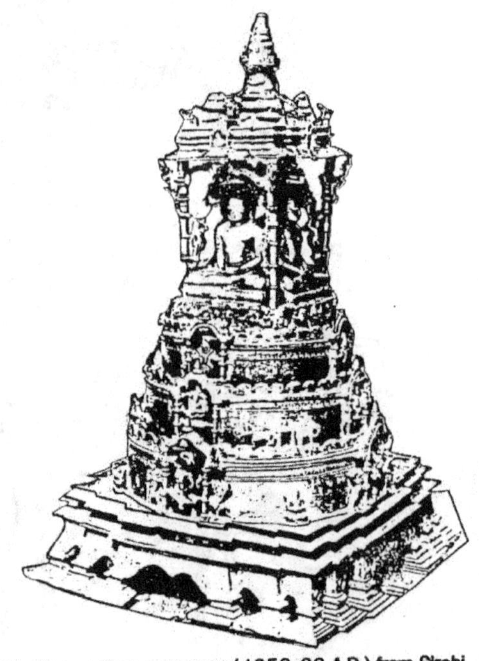

17. Bronze Samavasaraṇa (1053-60 A.D.) from Sirohi

9 798648 992825